THE SECRETS OF
the PYRAMIDS

A MESSAGE FOR HUMANITY

The Secrets Of The Pyramids - A Message For Humanity
By Michael Feeley

Published 2017 by Sazmick Books
Web: www.sazmickbooks.com
Web: www.michael-feeley.com

Book and Cover Design - Sarah Feeley, Sazmick Books

British Library Cataloguing-in Publication Data.
A catalogue record for this book is available from the British Library.

ISBN: 978-0-9954554-4-3

Printed and bound in the UK
using sustainable resources

THE SECRETS OF the PYRAMIDS
A MESSAGE FOR HUMANITY

MICHAEL FEELEY

SAZMICK BOOKS

THE BOOK OF CONSCIOUSNESS

A SOUL SCIENCE

THE GREAT SECRETS REVEALED

THE RIDDLE

"What walks on four legs in the morning, two legs in the
afternoon, three legs in the evening, and no legs at night?"

If you answered the riddle of the Sphinx correctly – You may
now enter... You may now know the secrets of life!

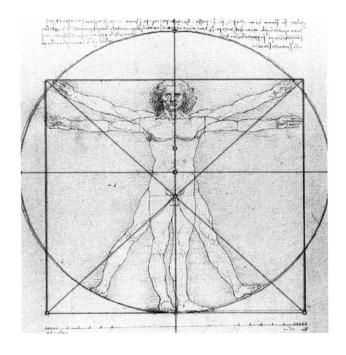

"The workings of the human body are an analogy for the workings of the universe."

- Leonardo da Vinci (1452 – 1519)

"Symbols are very adept at hiding the truth"

– Dan Brown; author of the Da Vinci Code

ACKNOWLEDGEMENTS

As always any acknowledgements must quite rightly begin with my beautiful wife Sarah and the beautiful 'G' for without their support this path would be much more difficult and rocky as I crawl up the stairs, playing drums on all of them with my feet, before I clumsily fall into bed and switch on the cold and worn out metallically loud sounding oscillating fan in the early hours of the morning; after much time-consuming research, with an eagerness to wake her up and tell all, to the sound of groans of insomnia. The next day of course being asked ''what did you tell me last night, it sounded interesting''? Can I also thank Gary D Purifory, for his foreword in this book, who I met after being invited to do one show on his 'Metaphysical Talk Radio show' which has now turned into 5 and counting. And finally can I thank whoever and whatever has entrusted me with this esoteric information as its guardian and keeper and its facilitator...

CONTENTS

FOREWORD

By Gary D Purifory – Former US Police Detective & Now Global Radio
Broadcaster at 'Metaphysical Talk Radio'

Egyptology and The Great Pyramids have mystified us all for a countless number of years. When we think of Ancient Egypt, we think of Pharaohs, Moses and the Israelites, and other such stories about Mummies, plagues, and so-on.

But for the serious-minded researcher, Egyptology represents so much more than the stories that have been derived from that great culture. The history that we've been taught in our classrooms growing up neither gave us a creditable and/or a serious look at a culture whose influence has far reached beyond the boundaries of time, and into our world today.

When I personally began to study Egyptology (on a serious level), the place to start for me was with the Great Pyramids. I discovered during this study that these great monolithic structures held the key to a message directed toward mankind, but my question was "from whom did this message come?".

Well, if there was even an individual whom I would readily endorse, and trust as an "investigator-of-facts", it would be the author of this book Mr. Michael Feeley. Like myself, Michael has utilized and incorporated many of the techniques and tools (he used as a law enforcement officer) to investigate and solve some the world's greatest of mysteries.

In his first endeavour; "The Secret of Christ" Michael effectively connected-the-dots to an age-old myth which has influenced mankind and his approach to faith, and how that "mindless" faith has led us all to a potentially disastrous end.

In this book, Michael once again gives us the "who-when-what-where-how-and-why" (a standard formula used in criminal investigations) regarding the Pyramids, and the coded message they embody. I've (on the record) stated regarding Michael's first book "that every human being should read". I echo the very same appeal here as well. Every human being should read what Michael discloses regarding the mysteries of the Great Pyramids.

The information Michael has shared in the past, has made for great radio listening that (in fact) spanned over multiple episodes of interviews. I am convinced that this book will not only ignite the interest of many, but also answer many "unanswered" questions we all may have regarding the coded messages which lies within the Great Pyramids.

Gary D. Purifory
Co-Owner/Program Director
Metaphysical Talk Radio
Host of "Progress for Tomorrow" Radio Show

ABOUT THE AUTHOR

Michael Feeley is an ex-police officer from the UK who has 17 years of investigative experience. For most of this time he was engaged in evidential factual writing for court purposes, securing evidence and presenting it to the appropriate departments and people in a matter of fact, succinct and to the point format. This style has survived with him. He is also a descendent of ancient Irish Celtic Kings.

It is believed that the Egyptian Princess Meritamun meaning 'Beloved of Amun' who was the daughter of Nefertiti and Akhenaten and the sister of Tutankhamun left Egypt and settled in the British Isles. It is from this genetic line that the Celtic Kings of Ireland were created. Michael therefore has connections to both Irish Celtic Kings and the Egyptian Royal lineage.

In 2009 his life changed with a gigantic quantum leap as he was the subject of a multitude of strange paranormal and supernatural experiences that changed his view of reality and life forever and caused him to leave his secure 'job for life' career to delve into the then unknown with blind faith and trust. He had seen and experienced many things of the paranormal and supernatural kind including witnessing with his own eyes on two separate occasions dimensional gateways/portals opening up in front of him at ground level and also in the night sky above him.

From a very young age Michael knew that he was different in many ways, he had a passion to know the deeper meanings of the world and wider universe and finding many answers has enriched his life, a calling has been achieved. In Egyptian Michael derives from Mikal meaning Blue, representing the Sky/Astronomical knowledge of the ether/heaven; depicted by the Blue coloured Egyptian God Amun; Amun meaning hidden.

He wanted to know why people have systems of belief, why people have certain dates of significance like Christmas and why people engage themselves in these beliefs and practices. Michael is not religious and has no religious background, however he realised that there was a wonderful mystique and hidden language behind many of the stories and events and wanted to decipher its numerous meanings in both verse and building Architecture and how it stems back to ancient Egypt which is also one of Michael's passions. Egypt has always been influential and even the modern day symbols we see on a daily basis within Government and society generally derives from this great land.

He was shown numerous times a 'Golden Key' in his mind's eye meaning the key that unlocks secret knowledge and at one point his gaze was continuously drawn towards 'Oak Trees' standing alone in fields, so much so he couldn't remove that gaze, there was a deeper connection, maybe another key to open up something inside, a deep and distant memory. It is without coincidence that the people we know as the Druids came to the British Isles from the ancient Mystery schools of Egypt, the word Druid comes from Dru-Id which means Oak Knowledge! In essence Tree knowledge that connects to the word True knowledge, nothing is coincidental. The Druids were the Djedhi of Egypt and were initiates of the Egyptian mystery schools of advanced knowledge, they were the enlightened serpents.

He has now found many of the answers to the origins of beliefs and religions and how these systems are really referring to a much deeper truth hidden cleverly by symbols and superficial stories that have occupied the minds of billions for many millenniums. Michael is now sharing the origins of these systems so that people can understand the intricate web woven around them to deliberately keep them as far away from the truth as possible by a small group of people who wish to keep this valuable truth to themselves for personal gain and control.

Many of the revelations (Revelation meaning to share hidden knowledge with humanity) came to Michael as an idea, a theory, but then when he looked into the idea everything pointed him in the direction that he was correct. It was the

Eureka moment that transpired into fact. The Great mysteries of our time and many that had gone before it had now for him been solved.

Prepare for many hidden secrets to be revealed to you that were only previously known by a select few chosen initiates who have kept a wondrous knowledge to themselves for far too long!

Michael is a trained investigator of uncovering evidential facts and the contents of this book are what he has painstakingly discovered, with the help from those who wanted him to discover it. During the writing of this book Michael has seen serpents of light swirling around his left foot and a cobalt blue Scarab beetle manifesting out of thin air in the living room of his house as he lay there contemplating the meaning of life, as he often does, being the thinking man.

Prepare to be enlightened the Egyptian way by virtue of the Egyptian principles of the 'All within All'...

INTRODUCTION

Egypt is an instant image forming name, the Pyramids, the Sphinx and mummies and hieroglyphs, to name but a few. However the word Egypt is the Greek name for this land deriving from the word Aegyptos.

Egypt was originally known as Khem, meaning the Black Earth or Black Lands, but that is the topic of debate and gives rise to such words we use frequently today like Chemistry and Chemical and Alchemy. It is world famous with its magnificent monuments that have stood the test of time on the landscape for millions of visitors to see each year, myself included. Egyptologists and historians have given us a version of history based on guess work and a limited one dimensional viewpoint regarding their purpose. Tombs for the Pharaoh's, built by the Pharaoh's for themselves assisted by slaves working with primitive tools able to transport rocks hundreds of tonnes in weight for miles over desert terrain!

But with all the versions of truth, with all the speculation, all of the so-called experts are missing one big point, whether that is deliberate to cover up the truth or whether it is out of a lack of understanding is yet to be established. But whichever scenario it is they are missing the point by more than a megalithic yard or an Egyptian Royal Cubit; but in fact by many miles.

To understand the true meaning of these great monuments you need to look beyond their magnificence and understand the mind of an advanced race with advanced knowledge that they have left us encoded within their monuments. Only then can you begin to understand what they knew, what they were telling us about us and how we too can become advanced like them. Their knowledge has been kept concealed by a select few elite families since the ancient Egyptian mystery schools and they have used that knowledge to further themselves and their own influence globally even today.

They have in effect stolen our rightful inheritance which is knowledge and now it is time for us to take it back from the secret halls such as Masonic halls and put it back into the public domain for everyone where it belongs.

The Egyptians believed that knowledge was a privilege and not a right however if you are reading this, you have been deemed privileged to know these true secrets of self, just as I have been privileged to have been allowed to learn them and share them. Enlightenment will come about with the re-emergence (or the emergence of RE-The Etheric Consciousness) of Egyptian knowledge (knowledge means to know) and this book contributes in some way to that awakening process.

In 2010 just prior to myself and my wife visiting Egypt for a 14 day holiday I was emailed out of the blue by someone unknown to me. She was a psychic medium from Scotland who had an important message for me and also my wife Sarah (Sa-Ra(h) = Protected by RA).

That email stated that a messenger would be there to meet us (albeit it turned out not to be a physical one) and that I was to look passed the tourism of Egypt, learn her secrets, understand them and then teach them. That message is now only beginning to make sense 7 years later, after many hours, many days, many months and many years of searching. I am also continually seeing the number 22. The mathematical formula of the approximation for π is 22/7. 22/7 = 3.1428571 which is an approximation of PI itself; which is also significant in the mathematical coordinates of the Pyramids and other ancient monuments, which I will also touch upon later in greater detail. When you consider the creator of the universe to be a supreme mathematician it makes sense that such a mathematician would speak to us by numbers. 22 is also the number of letters in the Egyptian hieroglyphic alphabet.

THE 22 LETTERS OF THE EGYPTIAN HIEROGLYPHIC ALPHABET

Egypt is forever influential even in today's modern society and that influence will became apparent in a later chapter, albeit sometimes hidden in plain sight for us to decipher or usually to completely miss.

You are about to read and learn and understand the missing link that so many famous explorers and alike have clearly missed, the secret teachings and the secret codes left for us to find.

Enjoy what you are about to read. You are amongst the privileged who are ready to know!

The book will take you through the origin of religious characters such as Jesus and who/what he really is, and it will describe the ancient knowledge based system that formed these belief systems. And the book will conclude with the knowledge of the most advanced race the world has ever known, a race so advanced that their legacy and their message is visited by millions of tourists each year who have no clue just what it is that they are looking at and what message is being attempted by monumental incommunicado, not even the scholars, Egyptologists or even the local populous know.

But after all this time I now know their secrets and it is my honour and privilege to be the facilitator of this ancient message that has waited for so long to be passed on; wanting to help people, a message held in suspended animation, dating back to a time when our distant genetic relatives walked the Earth, trying to speak with us and help us to reach our true God-like potential.

YOUR POTENTIAL GREATNESS:

ENLIGHTENMENT: A Dictionary Definition:

The action of enlightening or the state of being enlightened.
Enlightenment is a profound emotional and spiritual experience accompanied by feelings of ecstasy in which an individual transcends normal consciousness and receives realizations and truths about their reason for being and the true nature of reality which are not easily expressed in words but must be achieved through personal revelation. Enlightenment can be achieved by preparing through meditative techniques and study of spiritual texts which prepares the mind for its experience. People who seek out enlightenment are normally spiritually unsatisfied by modern day religion and seek a profound personal experience with the ultimate truth. The explanation of enlightenment can only be defined by one that has attained enlightenment. Therefore enlightenment is beyond comprehension from the human consciousness of an unenlightened individual. It transcends anything beyond human comprehension unless an individual has attained enlightenment.

CONSCIOUSNESS: A Dictionary Definition:

Consciousness is the state or quality of awareness, or, of being aware of an external object or something within oneself. It has been defined variously in terms of sentience, awareness, subjectivity, the ability to experience or to feel, wakefulness, having a sense of selfhood or soul, the fact that there is something "that it is like" to "have" or "be" it, and the executive control system of the mind, or the state or quality of awareness, or, of being aware of an external object or something within oneself. In contemporary philosophy its definition is often hinted at via the logical possibility of its absence, the philosophical zombie, which is defined as a being whose behavior and function are identical to one's own yet there is "no-one in there" experiencing it.

KUNDALINI AWAKENING: A Dictionary Definition:

Kundalini, in the concept of Dharma, refers to a form of primal energy said to be located at the base of the spine. Different spiritual traditions teach methods of "awakening" kundalini for the purpose of reaching spiritual enlightenment and a range of supernormal powers. Writer Joseph Campbell describes the concept of Kundalini as "the figure of a coiled female serpent—a serpent goddess not of "gross" but of "subtle" substance - which is to be thought of as residing in a torpid, slumbering state in a subtle centre, the first of the seven, near the base of the spine: the aim of the yoga then being to rouse this serpent, lift her head, and bring her up a subtle nerve or channel of the spine to the so-called "thousand-petaled lotus" at the crown of the head.

She, rising from the lowest to the highest lotus centre, will pass through and wake the five between, and with each waking the psychology and personality of the practitioner will be altogether and fundamentally transformed."

It is a transfer of energy.

Not many people on this planet know what you will know at the end of this book.

So in 21st century speak; You have 1 new message...

OBJECTIVES OF THE BOOK:

* Introduction to the author.

* Information on the Mainstream Version of Egypt.

* Introduction to the Gods of Egypt.

* Inform about the Egyptian Roots of Royalty and Government.

* Expose Zecharia Sitchen and an alternative interpretation of the Sumerian Scrolls.

* Highlight just a few of the Egyptian symbology in modern society (usually missed).

* Teach of The Real Reasons for the Pyramids & Sphinx (Advanced knowledge).

* To Reveal the true Identities of such characters as Jesus Christ; Moses, Adam & Eve; Mother Mary Et Al.

* To Recite The Lord's Prayer giving an Esoteric translation.

* The New Age – Why it's Not the road to Enlightenment.

* Demonstrate The Pyramid Matrix – A Monumental Mathematical Connection between all Earthly ancient cultures and also intergalactic.

* How The Establishment Keeps You From Knowing Advanced Knowledge.

* To Show That Religions And Various Global Cultures Are All Talking About The Same Thing; The Human Body and the Human Mind.

"Michael; regarding your trip to Egypt!
You need to first look passed the tourism, learn about her, understand her and then teach about her "

This was a coded message sent to me by a UK Psychic Medium a week prior to my trip to Egypt – I had never known her or even spoken to her until she contacted me with this message; it came entirely out of the blue! (Name Protected)

1

OUR EGYPTIAN HOLIDAY
(Michael & Sarah's Holy-day)

From Cairo To Biro

Where shall we go on holiday this year? I'm getting a strong pull towards Egypt! Let's book it and also some good trips whist we're there. We have to go to the Pyramids and Cairo Museum, that's a must otherwise there's no point, if you go to Egypt you have to go there. The holiday is now booked, trips arranged the first one being a 4am internal flight to Cairo for a toured guide around the famous sights. The day arrives and we make our way to Birmingham airport for the 6 hour flight to Egypt followed by a two week vacation, in sweltering winter heat.

Through security without a hitch and onto the plane, the metallic cigar above hundreds of clouds that rest below us, pushed along in an orderly manner by an etheric wind; as our child-like excitement flies with us alongside our tubular craft. All the build-up and all the advice about Mosquito spray was now behind us as we eventually landed on Egyptian soil. A new adventure and a new chapter in our lives to talk about forever more and a new experience that could never be forgotten. A spiritual new age phase for us that painted a wrong picture, answers and explanations that were ultimately wrong, but at the time we were in a state of Karast, the sleep-state, a mind that was unliberated.

1

We had arranged to go quad-biking in the Sinai desert, the fabled land of Moses, we had arranged to go scuba diving in the Red Sea and we had arranged to stay with the Bedouin people in the desert itself, all of which we did after the day in Cairo. 3am alarm, week one, we need to get ready for our flight to Cairo, we're being picked up from the hotel in the next hour, eyes glazed but held open by the tetrahedron thoughts of a never to be forgotten day. Now outside we await transport in the Egyptian Apophis, but as transport arrives it's not a limousine but an old car that looked like it belonged on the set of the 70's hit police show the Sweeney, as telegraph poles signalled the morning call to Mosques everywhere near!

The plummet of black smoke from the exhaust pipe as bang after bang, back-fire after back-fire our transport gently stopped and we both got in. This was not the kind of time travel I had expected. A short trip to the airport followed by a short 40 minute flight to Cairo, which was better and more appealing than the alternative 9 hour air-conless coach trip by road by any means, the plane was our chosen means of travel.

The density of the city of Cairo soon hit us with cars bumper to bumper and the sound of horns giving us that ambient music of this Afro-Asiatic land, much worse than daily rush hour on London's M25.

And of course not forgetting the cattle running between us and Horse drawn carriages overtaking at every possible opportunity dangerously missing moving cars by a fractal of a second and a crash wounded coat of auto-paint. The Museum was next on the itinerary after a trip down the River Nile for a spot of lunch with resident insects and our guide Mohammed (Meaning Praiseworthy) gave us many funny stories on the way. Antiquities everywhere and a sense that we may even bump into the legendry and world famous hat-wearing Egyptologist Dr Zahi Hawas but unfortunately with no eventual encounter; it has to be said. A challenge was made to me by museum staff, calling me Arnie, due to my wide western shoulders, the challenge to rip some Egyptian papyrus in exchange for 100 camels if I were to be successful, which I was, but I was never given my camels and never had to pay the excess baggage charge that would have been administered by our airline had I have claimed my rightful prize, obviously some sort of Pyramid Scheme. Ancient 3000 year old Pharaonic Mummies that looked better than I did due to the early start and long journey I had taken that day, lay waiting for us to view them, my eyes had travelled through time to connect with ancient times; but they were met with a distant vision far too out-there to imagine that I was looking at someone who had once walked the Earth as I now did, a feeling of humanitarian separation. After an exhausting heat blasting visit we boarded our awaiting coach and made our way to the Pyramids, more jokes and more mainstream versions of the Pyramids and the Sphinx and how and what their purpose was, seemingly wrong of course, but nevertheless a version of history (His-Story) repeated towards every seat and every visitor each and every day by a guide happy to tell all and tow the mainstream party line.

Then all of a sudden a familiar shape, a glimpse between decadent houses and high-rise flats and fast food restaurants to see a Pyramid, hardly splendour and magnificence, yet I had caught sight of the most ingenious monument planet Earth had ever witnessed being built, even though I didn't realise it at the time, only now 7 years on do I actually realise it!

My stomach didn't fill with emotion like I had expected instead it was silenced by an unusual calmness and stillness of everyday business, nothing out of the ordinary, but how could that be?

I was looking directly at human ancestral advancement by far greater than anything the modern day has to offer; monuments that I was told were built by the primitive tools of Hebrew slaves, utter non-sense of course but I had no better information to challenge that version, as yet.

We jumped off the coach landing on a million grains of sand, causing crystallised foot imprints like sole shaped fortress castle moats as we crunched and walked passed camels, beggars, other tourists and local Egyptians (from where we get the word Gypsies) wanting to do barter battle with iconic keep-sakes and not forgetting the corrupt policemen wanting money to take our photographs by way of deceptive means. A site tarnished by modern building developments that encircled the Pyramids with insolence and a lack of respect. But with awe and amazement we had finally reached our destination, a tetrahedron of stones placed with precision and pre-destined motive, the cutting of the stones a result of sound energy within the sound and resonance chambers of the pyramids themselves. But what was their reason, what was their purpose and what was mine? Maybe crawling on my knees along the low chambers and tunnel networks inside the Great Pyramid, the enemy of claustrophobia, may contain some answers.

A burial site for the Pharaoh's, no, definitely not, an extra-terrestrial landing site, it had been said, but no, I didn't get that feeling. The Lion guardian, the Sphinx, laughed at my multitude of guesses, all incorrect, but in my new age stage feelings were everything and I walked away satisfied of the answers. I now know better.

In hindsight what the trip did was to open up an aspect of me in readiness for now, as mentioned in the introduction of this book I was told by a psychic medium before I even went, by email, that I had a purpose there, beyond a vacation, that I was to look passed her tourism, learn about her, understand her and then teach about her, her being Egypt.

But little did I realise that hundreds of hours research later, hundreds of different routes taken and hundreds of thoughts now captured in universal archives as a genetic trace, I now look passed the tourism, I now understand her and I now teach about her and the message that she sends to assist us even now in the 21st century of human existence. It has taken me 7 years to arrive at the correct station after much mindful journeying and much mental travelling.

From the hidden remnants of Egypt to the knowledge thirsty glass of your life; I have a message for you that has patiently waited 10,000 years to find you!

The Ankh awaits your presence at the table of Kings, you have a reservation there!

2

EGYPT; THE MAINSTREAM VERSION

Great Pyramids of Giza

"No pyramids are more celebrated than the Great Pyramids of Giza, located on a plateau on the west bank of the Nile River, on the outskirts of modern-day Cairo; the oldest and largest of the three pyramids at Giza, known as the Great Pyramid, is the only surviving structure out of the famed seven wonders of the ancient world. It was built for Khufu (Cheops, in Greek), Sneferu's successor and the second of the eight kings of the fourth dynasty.

Though Khufu reigned for 23 years (2589-2566 B.C.), relatively little is known of his reign beyond the grandeur of his pyramid. The sides of the pyramid's base average 755.75 feet (230 meters), and its original height was 481.4 feet (147 meters), making it the largest pyramid in the world. Three small pyramids built for Khufu's queens are lined up next to the Great Pyramid, and a tomb was found nearby containing the empty sarcophagus of his mother, Queen Hetepheres. Like other pyramids, Khufu's is surrounded by rows of mastabas, where relatives or officials of the king were buried to accompany and support him in the afterlife.

The middle pyramid at Giza was built for Khufu's son Khafre (2558-2532 B.C). A unique feature built inside Khafre's pyramid complex was the Great Sphinx, a guardian statue carved in limestone with the head of a man and the body of a lion. It was the largest statue in the ancient world, measuring 240 feet long and 66 feet high. In the 18th dynasty (c. 1500 B.C.) the Great Sphinx would come to be worshiped itself, as the image of a local form of the god Horus. The southernmost pyramid at Giza was built for Khafre's son

Menkaure (2532-2503 B.C.). It is the shortest of the three pyramids (218 feet) and is a precursor of the smaller pyramids that would be constructed during the fifth and sixth dynasties.

Approximately 2.3 million blocks of stone (averaging about 2.5 tons each) had to be cut, transported and assembled to build Khufu's Great Pyramid. The ancient Greek historian Herodotus wrote that it took 20 years to build and required the labour of 100,000 men, but later archaeological evidence suggests that the workforce might actually have been around 20,000.
Though some popular versions of history held that the pyramids were built by slaves or foreigners forced into labour, skeletons excavated from the area show that the workers were probably native Egyptian agricultural labourers who worked on the pyramids during the time of year when the Nile River flooded much of the land nearby". Courtesy of www.history.com

End of mainstream narrative!

Authors Note- 'For this to be the case slaves would have to have worked 24/7 moving one brick per second for 20 years continuously!

It is impossible to deny that they were built, they are there for all to see and therefore they have to have been built. Maybe there is evidence of slave labour as this mainstream chapter suggests.

However I am denying the mainstream version of their purpose. That purpose as you will see in the forthcoming chapters far exceeds simple burial plots for the aristocracy and it far exceeds a simple grand design to mark a grand send-off, there is an advanced knowledge speaking to us.

Pharaohs yes, they had influential involvement; they held secret knowledge as did the priests to the point of self-aggrandisement. Knowledge that they protected for themselves and those worthy of its inheritance; themselves and certain chosen initiates.

No Pharaoh has ever been found buried within the Pyramids and that is for good reason. .

Cairo/al-Qāhirah means Coptic and optic means belonging or relating to a part of the Christian Church which was started in Egypt. If we look at the helicopter drawn on Egyptian stone in Abydos that looks like a modern day helicopter may be this is telling us about the Heli (Helios/sun) Copter (Coptics) together meaning 'Christian Egyptian'.

Many modern day religions have their origin in Egypt with the likes of

Christianity and its Sun worship; for example 'Church Bells'. Bel was a Canaanite Sun-God (god of sunset, the equivalent of the Egyptian sun-god Set).

The mainstream is not telling you all there is to know... please read on!'

3

THE GODS OF EGYPT

The Egyptians worshipped many Gods and Goddesses and the mainstream has its own version of the meanings and what they stood for. This is not entirely correct, there is a much deeper meaning to these Gods and Goddesses and although they were aplenty I have listed a few of them below with a brief summary only at this stage as I reference them throughout the book giving their real meanings.

Horus was the Sun at dawn, from where we get the word Horizon meaning Horus –Risen. It is also where we get the word Hour(s) (Horus anagram) in our time system, where is the Sun now, what Hour (Horus) is it? The clock is representative of the Sun (hour) Moon (Minutes) and Mercury which has the fastest Orbit around the Sun (Seconds on the clock).

RA was the visible Sun at its Zenith at 12 noon. (RA in astronomical coordinates means 'Right Ascension'). RA in Egyptian language simply translates as Sun.

Set was the Sun at Sunset (Sun-Set) and is where we get George of St George and the Dragon fame which I will go into later.

Osiris (Orion constellation) was the Sun below your feet hence God of the Underworld. He is referenced throughout this book and especially when we get to the Egyptian chapter, so I won't spoil anything now. He was also known as the 'God of the Staircase' - a staircase having seven steps; which refers to the Chakra system along the spine.

Isis/Sophis meaning Wisdom (Sophis = sophisticated) (astronomically Sirius 'A' & Lunar Moon) is the Goddess of Fertility and the original Mother Mary, who is the Christianised version of this Goddess (Horus was the original Jesus). She is also referenced in the Egyptian section as having a much more esoteric meaning. The word sister derives from Isis-star, and as Leonardo Da Vinci told us in his famous painting; the Mona Lisa; is that Mona (Old English for Moon) is L'isa (Isis) Mona Lisa = Isis Moon.

Nephthys, meaning invisible sister is the sister of Isis (she is Sirius B in a planetary sense).Sirius means 'Burning' or 'Scorching'.

Thoth, the God of Wisdom, is in esoteric meanings; Thought! Which is applicable later in the Egyptian consciousness chapter.

Neteru is the Goddess of nature. When we talk about nature it goes beyond the trees and plants it also refers to the higher forces of nature, the ether and extends into original creation itself.

Ma'at, the Goddess of balance which also extends to the universal balance, the chaos theory and underlying order within natural phenomenon. Ma'at also means mother & father which again is balancing of opposites, masculine and feminine.

Wadjet, the Goddess and ruler of lower Egypt (North of the Nile Delta) and protector of Royalty. She is seen on the headdress of many Pharaohs.

Nehkbet is Goddess and ruler of Upper Egypt (South of the Nile Delta) She is also featured on the headdress of the likes of Tutankhamun. She was also known as a Vulture goddess. The Vulture in Egypt represented femininity an maternal protection. She later became an heraldic symbol of upper Egypt.

There were of course many other Egyptian Gods and Goddess all with an esoteric meaning not widely taught but for now these are the ones dealt with in this book.

Anubis; which means 'Royal Child' who escorted the soul/spirit into the afterlife, the consciousness journey after mummification, symbolic of the soul's embodiment into a physical body, universal consciousness that became unconscious as physical matter.

Ptah was the chief Egyptian deity accredited with the creation of the universe and all things. Ptah gives us the word father and is referred to in this book as the 'Black light' the ether and the dark matter.

There were also the Cat-Goddess such as Sekmet. Cats were also revered in Egypt as they can see into the two worlds, the physical and metaphysical (afterlife) which is why there are so many cat goddess in Egyptian writings. Cats are also seen as the feminine forces of Nature.

This has been a short insight into the famous Gods of Egypt, but as I've said, there is a much deeper esoteric meaning that often gets overlooked, either intentionally or otherwise. It is a hidden pictorial message that reveals itself with knowledge and understanding of its dialogue.

4

THE EGYPTIAN ROOTS OF ROYALTY AND GOVERNMENT

The whole concept of Royalty and Sovereign ruler-ship derives from Egypt. Royal, meaning the God-King, a title given to the Pharaoh's of Egypt as they were believed to possess Godlike attributes, the walking Gods on Earth.

Bloodline marriages were the norm to ensure that their DNA remained pure, a family match of incest, just like the Royalty of today who despite mainstream media falsities claiming otherwise; like Kate Middleton being a commoner; when she is actually the cousin of her husband Prince William.

Royal DNA cannot go outside of family ties, ever, it is their law of purity. Their coronations involve oils, which is where we get the word anointed,

which means to oil (This also has Jesus connotations which I go into later). Men bow down to Royalty which means to yield and submit and women curtsey which derives from courtesy. It is a form of worship or veneration, veneration meaning the act of honouring a saint; a person who has been identified as having a high degree of sanctity or holiness.

(Above: Prince William)

Saint derives from Sanctus meaning holy. Amun was considered the most holy

17

of Egyptian Gods and this is significant later when I discuss Amun which means Hidden and also the monotheistic God Aten and the sanctity of self. All American Presidents, bar one, has been related to the Pharaoh's of Egypt, European Royalty and even into the British government; it is a royal bloodline symbolised by the Red carpet at such events as the Oscars. It is a Genetic line unbroken for aeons of time; the Genesis meaning the Gene of Isis. Isis means 'She of the throne' and all things royal stem from these ancient times and this famous culture.

(Above: Queen of England on the Egyptian symbolic Throne; throne is the throne of God, the higher chakras and the physical crown is symbolic of the crown chakra which I will go into later)

When the current Queen of England, Elizabeth II, Elizabeth meaning Oath of God or Pledged to God (Oath = formal promise); was coronated she underwent a ritual that encompassed Hebrew, Roman/Latin; Christian, Judaic and Egyptian principles. They are ultimately the same thing and are closely interwoven and interconnected, borrowed from the Egyptian rituals themselves by these other cultures. This is the whole service from beginning to end:

Note the many references that will come up many times throughout the book, and note that the ceremony itself is an elite form of language set above the vocabulary of most people because they view themselves of higher grace that the common untitled person:

The Coronation of Queen Elizabeth II: Different Sections of the Ceremony:

The Preparation
In the morning upon the day of the Coronation early, care is to be taken that

the Ampulla be filled with Oil for the anointing, and, together with the Spoon, be laid ready upon the Altar in the Abbey Church.

The LITANY shall be sung as the Dean and Prebendaries and the choir of Westminster proceed from the Altar to the west door of the Church.

The Archbishops being already vested in their Copes and Mitres and the Bishops Assistant in their Copes, the procession shall be formed immediately outside of the west door of the Church, and shall wait till notice be given of the approach of her Majesty, and shall then begin to move into the Church.

And the people shall remain standing from the Entrance until the beginning of the Communion Service.

II. The Entrance into the Church

The Queen, as soon as she enters at the west door of the Church, is to be received with this Anthem:

Psalm 122, 1–3, 6, 7.

I was glad when they said unto me:
We will go into the house of the Lord.
Our feet shall stand in thy gates:
O Jerusalem.
Jerusalem is built as a city:
that is at unity in itself.
O pray for the peace of Jerusalem:
they shall prosper that love thee.
Peace be within thy walls:
and plenteousness within thy palaces.

The Queen shall in the meantime pass up through the body of the Church, into and through the choir, and so up the steps to the Theatre; and having passed by her Throne, she shall make her humble adoration, and then kneeling at the faldstool set for her before her Chair of Estate on the south side of the Altar, use some short private prayers; and after, sit down in her Chair.

The Bible, Paten, and Chalice shall meanwhile be brought by the Bishops who had borne them, and placed upon the Altar.

Then the Lords who carry in procession the Regalia, except those who carry the Swords, shall come from their places and present in order everyone what he carries to the Archbishop, who shall deliver them to the Dean of Westminster, to be placed by him upon the Altar.

III. The Recognition

The Archbishop, together with the Lord Chancellor, Lord Great Chamberlain, Lord High Constable, and Earl Marshal (Garter King of Arms preceding them), shall then go to the East side of the Theatre, and after shall go to the other three sides in this order, South, West, and North, and at every of the four sides the Archbishop shall with a loud voice speak to the People: and the Queen in the meanwhile, standing up by King Edward's Chair, shall turn and show herself unto the People at every of the four sides of the Theatre as the Archbishop is at every of them, the Archbishop saying:

"Sirs, I here present unto you
Queen ELIZABETH,
your undoubted Queen:
Wherefore all you who are come this day
to do your homage and service,
Are you willing to do the same?"

The People signify their willingness and joy, by loud and repeated acclamations, all with one voice crying out,

"GOD SAVE QUEEN ELIZABETH."

Then the trumpets shall sound.

IV. The Oath

The Queen having returned to her Chair (her Majesty having already on Tuesday, the fourth day of November, 1952, in the presence of the two Houses of Parliament, made and signed the Declaration prescribed by Act of Parliament), the Archbishop standing before her shall administer the Coronation Oath, first asking the Queen,

"Madam, is your Majesty willing to take the Oath?"

And the Queen answering,
"I am willing,"
The Archbishop shall minister these questions; and the Queen, having a book

in her hands, shall answer each question severally as follows:

Archbishop: Will you solemnly promise and swear to govern the Peoples of the United Kingdom of Great Britain and Northern Ireland, Canada, Australia, New Zealand, the Union of South Africa, Pakistan and Ceylon, and of your Possessions and other Territories to any of them belonging or pertaining, according to their respective laws and customs?
Queen: I solemnly promise so to do.

Archbishop: Will you to your power cause Law and Justice, in Mercy, to be executed in all your judgements?

Queen: I will.

Archbishop: Will you to the utmost of your power maintain the Laws of God and the true profession of the Gospel?

Will you to the utmost of your power maintain in the United Kingdom the Protestant Reformed Religion established by law?

Will you maintain and preserve inviolably the settlement of the Church of England, and the doctrine, worship, discipline, and government thereof, as by law established in England?

And will you preserve unto the Bishops and Clergy of England, and to the Churches there committed to their charge, all such rights and privileges, as by law do or shall appertain to them or any of them?

Queen: All this I promise to do.

Then the Queen arising out of her Chair, supported as before, the Sword of State being carried before her, shall go to the Altar, and make her solemn Oath in the sight of all the people to observe the premises: laying her right hand upon the Holy Gospel in the great Bible (which was before carried in the procession and is now brought from the altar by the Archbishop, and tendered to her as she kneels upon the steps), and saying these words:

The things which I have here before promised, I will perform, and keep. So help me God.

Then the Queen shall kiss the Book and sign the Oath.
The Queen having thus taken her Oath shall return again to her Chair, and the

Bible shall be delivered to the Dean of Westminster.

V. The Presenting of the Holy Bible

When the Queen is again seated, the Archbishop shall go to her Chair; and the Moderator of the General Assembly of the Church of Scotland, receiving the Bible from the Dean of Westminster, shall bring it to the Queen and present it to her, the Archbishop saying these words:

Our gracious Queen:
to keep your Majesty ever mindful of the law and the Gospel of God
as the Rule for the whole life and government of Christian Princes,
we present you with this Book,
the most valuable thing that this world affords.

And the Moderator shall continue:
Here is Wisdom;
This is the royal Law;
These are the lively Oracles of God.

Then shall the Queen deliver back the Bible to the Moderator, who shall bring it to the Dean of Westminster, to be reverently placed again upon the Altar. This done, the Archbishop shall return to the Altar.

VI. The Beginning of the Communion Service

The Introit

Psalm 84, 9, 10.
Behold, O God our defender:
and look upon the face of thine Anointed.
For one day in thy courts:
is better than a thousand.

Then, the Queen with the people kneeling, the Archbishop shall begin the Communion Service saying:

Almighty God,
unto whom all hearts be open,
all desires known,
and from whom no secrets are hid:
Cleanse the thoughts of our hearts

by the inspiration of thy Holy Spirit,
that we may perfectly love thee,
and worthily magnify thy holy Name;
through Christ our Lord. Amen.

Archbishop: Lord have mercy upon us.
Answer: Christ have mercy upon us.
Archbishop: Lord have mercy upon us.

LET US PRAY

O God,
who providest for thy people by thy power,
and rulest over them in love:
Grant unto this thy servant ELIZABETH, our Queen,
the Spirit of wisdom and government,
that being devoted unto thee with her whole heart,
she may so wisely govern,
that in her time thy Church may be in safety,
and Christian devotion may continue in peace;
that so persevering in good works unto the end,
she may by thy mercy come to thine everlasting kingdom;
through Jesus Christ, thy Son, our Lord,
who liveth and reigneth with thee
in the unity of the Holy Ghost,
one God for ever and ever. Amen.

The Epistle

1 S. Peter 2, 13.
To be read by one of the Bishops.

Submit yourselves to every ordinance of man for the Lord's sake: whether it be
to the king, as supreme; or unto governors, as unto them that are sent by him
for the punishment of evildoers, and for the praise of them that do well. For so
is the will of God, that with well doing ye may put to silence the ignorance of
foolish men: as free, and not using your liberty for a cloke of maliciousness,
but as the servants of God. Honour all men. Love the brotherhood. Fear God.
Honour the king.

The Gradual
Psalm 141, 2.

Let my prayer come up into thy presence as the incense:
and let the lifting up of my hands be as an evening sacrifice. Alleluia.

The Gospel

S. Matthew 22, 15.
To be read by another Bishop, the Queen with the people standing.

Then went the Pharisees, and took counsel how they might entangle him in his talk. And they sent out unto him their disciples, with the Herodians, saying, Master, we know that thou art true, and teachest the way of God in truth, neither carest thou for any man: for thou regardest not the person of men. Tell us therefore, What thinkest thou? Is it lawful to give tribute unto Cæsar, or not? But Jesus perceived their wickedness, and said, Why tempt ye me, ye hypocrites? Shew me the tribute-money. And they brought unto him a penny. And he saith unto them, Whose is this image and superscription? They say unto him, Cæsar's. Then saith he unto them, Render therefore unto Cæsar the things which are Cæsar's: and unto God the things that are God's. When they had heard these words they marvelled, and left him, and went their way.

And the Gospel ended shall be sung the Creed following, the Queen with the people standing, as before.

I believe in one God,
the Father Almighty,
maker of heaven and earth,
And of all things visible and invisible;

And in one Lord Jesus Christ,
the only-begotten Son of God,
Begotten of his Father before all worlds,
God of God, Light of Light,
Very God of very God,
Begotten, not made,
Being of one substance with the Father,
By whom all things were made:
Who for us men, and for our salvation
came down from heaven,
and was incarnate by the Holy Ghost of the Virgin Mary,
And was made man;
And was crucified also for us under Pontius Pilate.
He suffered and was buried;

And the third day he rose again
according to the Scriptures,
And ascended into heaven,
And sitteth on the right hand of the Father.
And he shall come again with glory
to judge both the quick and the dead:
Whose kingdom shall have no end.

And I believe in the Holy Ghost,
The Lord and giver of life,
Who proceedeth from the Father and the Son,
Who with the Father and the Son together
is worshipped and glorified,
Who spake by the Prophets.
And I believe one Catholick and Apostolick Church.
I acknowledge one Baptism for the remission of sins.
And I look for the resurrection of the dead,
And the life of the world to come. Amen.

The Anointing

The Creed being ended, the Queen kneeling at her faldstool, and the people kneeling in their places, the Archbishop shall begin the hymn, VENI, CREATOR SPIRITUS, and the choir shall sing it out.

Come, Holy Ghost, our souls inspire,
And lighten with celestial fire.
Thou the anointing Spirit art,
Who dost thy seven-fold gifts impart.

Thy blessed Unction from above
Is comfort, life, and fire of love.
Enable with perpetual light
The dulness of our blinded sight.

Anoint and cheer our soiled face
With the abundance of thy grace:
Keep far our foes, give peace at home;
Where thou art guide, no ill can come.

Teach us to know the Father, Son
And thee, of both, to be but One;

That, through the ages all along,
This may be our endless song:

Praise to thy eternal merit,
Father, Son, and Holy Spirit.

The hymn being ended, the Archbishop shall say:

LET US PRAY

O Lord and heavenly Father,
the exalter of the humble and the strength of thy chosen,
who by anointing with Oil didst of old
make and consecrate kings, priests, and prophets,
to teach and govern thy people Israel:
Bless and sanctify thy chosen servant ELIZABETH,
who by our office and ministry
is now to be anointed with this Oil,
Here the Archbishop is to lay his hand upon the Ampulla.
and consecrated Queen:
Strengthen her, O Lord, with the Holy Ghost the Comforter;
Confirm and stablish her with thy free and princely Spirit,
the Spirit of wisdom and government,
the Spirit of counsel and ghostly strength,
the Spirit of knowledge and true godliness,
and fill her, O Lord, with the Spirit of thy holy fear,
now and for ever;
through Jesus Christ our Lord. Amen.

This prayer being ended, and the people standing, the choir shall sing:

I Kings 1, 39, 40.
Zadok the priest and Nathan the prophet anointed Solomon king;
and all the people rejoiced and said
God save the king,
Long live the king,
May the king live for ever. Amen. Hallelujah.

In the meantime, the Queen rising from her devotions, having been disrobed of her crimson robe by the Lord Great Chamberlain, assisted by the Mistress of the Robes, and being uncovered, shall go before the Altar, supported and attended as before.

The Queen shall sit down in King Edward's Chair (placed in the midst of the Area over against the Altar, with a faldstool before it), wherein she is to be anointed. Four Knights of the Garter shall hold over her a rich pall of silk, or cloth of gold: the Dean of Westminster, taking the Ampulla and Spoon from off the Altar, shall hold them ready, pouring some holy Oil into the Spoon, and with it the Archbishop shall anoint the Queen in the form of a cross:

On the palms of both the hands, saying,
Be thy Hands anointed with holy Oil.

On the breast, saying,
Be thy Breast anointed with holy Oil.

On the crown of the head, saying,
Be thy Head anointed with holy Oil:
as kings, priests, and prophets were anointed:

And as Solomon was anointed king
by Zadok the priest and Nathan the prophet,
so be thou anointed, blessed, and consecrated Queen
over the Peoples, whom the Lord thy God
hath given thee to rule and govern,
In the name of the Father, and of the Son, and of the Holy Ghost. Amen.

Then shall the Dean of Westminster lay the Ampulla and Spoon upon the Altar; and the Queen kneeling down at the faldstool, the Archbishop shall say this Blessing over her:
Our Lord Jesus Christ,
the Son of God,
who by his Father was anointed with the Oil of gladness
above his fellows,
by his holy Anointing pour down upon your Head and Heart
the blessing of the Holy Ghost,
and prosper the works of your Hands:
that by the assistance of his heavenly grace
you may govern and preserve
the Peoples committed to your charge
in wealth, peace, and godliness;
and after a long and glorious course
of ruling a temporal kingdom
wisely, justly, and religiously,
you may at last be made partaker of an eternal kingdom,

through the same Jesus Christ our Lord. Amen.

This prayer being ended, the Queen shall arise and sit down again in King Edward's Chair, while the Knights of the Garter bear away the pall; whereupon the Queen arising, the Dean of Westminster, assisted by the Mistress of the Robes, shall put upon her Majesty the Colobium Sindonis and the Supertunica or Close Pall of cloth of gold, together with a Girdle of the same. Then shall the Queen again sit down; and after her, the people also.

The Presenting of the Spurs and Sword, and the Oblation of the said Sword

The Spurs shall be brought from the Altar by the Dean of Westminster, and delivered to the Lord Great Chamberlain; who, kneeling down, shall present them to the Queen, who forthwith sends them back to the Altar.

Then the Lord who carries the Sword of State, delivering to the Lord Chamberlain the said Sword (which is thereupon deposited in Saint Edward's Chapel) shall receive from the Lord Chamberlain, in lieu thereof, another Sword in a scabbard which he shall deliver to the Archbishop: and the Archbishop shall lay it on the Altar and say:

Hear our prayers, O Lord, we beseech thee,
and so direct and support thy servant
Queen ELIZABETH,
that she may not bear the Sword in vain;
but may use it as the minister of God
for the terror and punishment of evildoers,
and for the protection and encouragement of those that do well,
through Jesus Christ our Lord. Amen.

Then shall the Archbishop take the Sword from off the Altar, and (the Archbishop of York and the Bishops of London and Winchester assisting and going along with him) shall deliver it into the Queen's hands; and, the Queen holding it, the Archbishop shall say:

Receive this kingly Sword,
brought now from the Altar of God,
and delivered to you by the hands of us
the Bishops and servants of God, though unworthy.
With this sword do justice,
stop the growth of iniquity,

protect the holy Church of God,
help and defend widows and orphans,
restore the things that are gone to decay,
maintain the things that are restored,
punish and reform what is amiss,
and confirm what is in good order:
that doing these things you may be glorious in all virtue;
and so faithfully serve our Lord Jesus Christ in this life,
that you may reign for ever with him
in the life which is to come. Amen.

Then the Queen, rising up and going to the Altar, shall offer it there in the scabbard, and then return and sit down in King Edward's Chair: and the Peer, who first received the Sword, shall offer the price of it, namely, one hundred shillings, and having thus redeemed it, shall receive it from the Dean of Westminster, from off the Altar, and draw it out of the scabbard, and carry it naked before her Majesty during the rest of the solemnity.

Then the Archbishop of York and the Bishops who have assisted during the offering shall return to their places.

IX. The Investing with the Armills, the Stole Royal and the Robe Royal: and the Delivery of the Orb

Then the Dean of Westminster shall deliver the Armills to the Archbishop, who, putting them upon the Queen's wrists, shall say:

Receive the Bracelets of sincerity and wisdom,
both for tokens of the Lord's protection embracing you on every side;
and also for symbols and pledges
of that bond which unites you with your Peoples:
to the end that you may be strengthened in all your works
and defended against your enemies both bodily and ghostly,
through Jesus Christ our Lord. Amen.

Then the Queen arising, the Robe Royal or Pall of cloth of gold with the Stole Royal shall be delivered by the Groom of the Robes to the Dean of Westminster, and by him, assisted by the Mistress of the Robes, put upon the Queen, standing; the Lord Great Chamberlain fastening the clasps. Then shall the Queen sit down, and the Archbishop shall say:
Receive this Imperial Robe,
and the Lord your God endue you with knowledge and wisdom,

with majesty and with power from on high;
the Lord clothe you with the robe of righteousness,
and with the garments of salvation. Amen.

The Delivery of the Orb

Then shall the Orb with the Cross be brought from the Altar by the Dean of
Westminster and delivered into the Queen's right hand by the Archbishop,
saying:

Receive this Orb set under the Cross,
and remember that the whole world
is subject to the Power and Empire
of Christ our Redeemer.

Then shall the Queen deliver the Orb to the Dean of Westminster, to be by him
laid on the Altar.

X. The Investiture per annulum, et per sceptrum et baculum

Then the Keeper of the Jewel House shall deliver to the Archbishop the Queen's
Ring, wherein is set a sapphire and upon it a ruby cross: the Archbishop shall
put it on the fourth finger of her Majesty's right hand, and say:

Receive the Ring of kingly dignity,
and the seal of Catholic Faith:
and as you are this day
consecrated to be our Head and Prince,
so may you continue steadfastly
as the Defender of Christ's Religion;
that being rich in faith
and blessed in all good works,
you may reign with him who is the King of Kings,
to whom be the glory for ever and ever. Amen.

Then shall the Dean of Westminster bring the Sceptre with the Cross and the
Rod with the Dove to the Archbishop.

The Glove having been presented to the Queen, the Archbishop shall deliver
the Sceptre with the Cross into the Queen's right hand, saying:
Receive the Royal Sceptre, the ensign of kingly power and justice.

And then he shall deliver the Rod with the Dove into the Queen's left hand, and say:

Receive the Rod of equity and mercy.
Be so merciful
that you be not too remiss,
so execute justice
that you forget not mercy.
Punish the wicked,
protect and cherish the just,
and lead your people
in the way wherein they should go.

XI. The Putting on of the Crown (Symbolic of the Crown Chakra)

Then the people shall rise; and the Archbishop, standing before the Altar, shall take the Crown into his hands, and laying it again before him upon the Altar, he shall say:

O God the Crown of the faithful:
Bless we beseech thee this Crown,
and so sanctify thy servant ELIZABETH
upon whose head this day thou dost place it
for a sign of royal majesty,
that she may be filled by thine abundant grace
with all princely virtues:
through the King eternal Jesus Christ our Lord. Amen.

Then the Queen still sitting in King Edward's Chair, the Archbishop, assisted with other Bishops, shall come from the Altar: the Dean of Westminster shall bring the Crown, and the Archbishop taking it of him shall reverently put it upon the Queen's head. At the sight whereof the people, with loud and repeated shouts, shall cry,

GOD SAVE THE QUEEN

The Princes and Princesses, the Peers and Peeresses shall put on their coronets and caps, and the Kings of Arms their crowns; and the trumpets shall sound, and by a signal given, the great guns at the Tower shall be shot off.

The acclamation ceasing, the Archbishop shall go on, and say:

God crown you with a crown of glory and righteousness, that having a right faith and manifold fruit of good works, you may obtain the crown of an everlasting kingdom by the gift of him whose kingdom endureth for ever. Amen.

Then shall the choir sing:

Be strong and of a good courage:
keep the commandments of the Lord thy God, and walk in his ways.

And the people shall remain standing until after the Homage be ended.

XII. The Benediction

And now the Queen having been thus anointed and crowned, and having received all the ensigns of Royalty, the Archbishop shall solemnly bless her: and the Archbishop of York and all the Bishops, with the rest of the Peers and all the people, shall follow every part of the Benediction with a loud and hearty Amen.

The Lord bless you and keep you.
The Lord protect you in all your ways
and prosper all your handiwork. Amen.

The Lord give you faithful Parliaments and quiet Realms;
sure defence against all enemies;
fruitful lands and a prosperous industry;
wise counsellors and upright magistrates;
leaders of integrity in learning and labour;
a devout, learned and useful clergy;
honest peaceable and dutiful citizens. Amen.

May Wisdom and Knowledge be the Stability of your Times,
and the fear of the Lord your Treasure. Amen.

The Lord who hath made you Queen over these Peoples
give you increase of grace, honour and happiness in this world,
and make you partaker of his eternal felicity
in the world to come. Amen.

Then shall the Archbishop turn to the people and say:

And the same Lord God Almighty grant
that the Clergy and Nobles assembled here
for this great and solemn service,
and together with them all the Peoples of this Commonwealth,
fearing God, and honouring the Queen,
may by the gracious assistance of God's infinite goodness,
and by the vigilant care of his anointed servant,
our gracious Sovereign,
continually enjoy peace, plenty, and prosperity;
through Jesus Christ our Lord,
to whom, with the eternal Father, and God the Holy Ghost,
be glory in the Church,
world without end. Amen.

The Enthroning

Then shall the Queen go to her Throne, and be lifted up into it by the Archbishops and Bishops, and other Peers of the Kingdom; and being enthroned, or placed therein, all the Great Officers, those that bear the Swords and the Sceptres, and the Nobles that carried the other Regalia, shall stand round about the steps of the Throne; and the Archbishop, standing before the Queen, shall say:

Stand firm, and hold fast from henceforth
the seat and state of royal and imperial dignity,
which is this day delivered unto you,
in the Name and by the Authority of Almighty God,
and by the hands of us
the Bishops and servants of God, though unworthy.
And the Lord God Almighty,
whose ministers we are, and the stewards of his mysteries,
establish your Throne in righteousness,
that it may stand fast for evermore. Amen.

The Homage

The Exhortation being ended, all the Princes and Peers then present shall do their Fealty and Homage publicly and solemnly unto the Queen: and the Queen shall deliver her Sceptre with the Cross and the Rod with the Dove, to some one near to the Blood Royal, or to the Lords that carried them in the procession, or to any other that she pleaseth to assign, to hold them by her, till the Homage be ended.

And the Bishops that support the Queen in the procession may also ease her, by supporting the Crown, as there shall be occasion.

The Archbishop shall first ascend the steps of the Throne and kneel down before her Majesty, and the rest of the Bishops shall kneel in their places: and they shall do their Fealty together, for the shortening of the ceremony: and the Archbishop, placing his hands between the Queen's shall say:

I, Geoffrey, Archbishop of Canterbury
[and so every one of the rest,
I, N. Bishop of N.,
repeating the rest audibly after the Archbishop]
will be faithful and true,
and faith and truth will bear unto you,
our Sovereign Lady,
Queen of this Realm and Defender of the Faith,
and unto your heirs and successors according to law.
So help me God.

Then shall the Archbishop kiss the Queen's right hand. After which the Duke of Edinburgh shall ascend the steps of the Throne, and having taken off his coronet, shall kneel down before her Majesty, and placing his hands between the Queen's shall pronounce the words of Homage, saying:

I, Philip, Duke of Edinburgh
do become your liege man of life and limb,
and of earthly worship;
and faith and truth I will bear unto you,
to live and die, against all manner of folks.
So help me God.

And arising, he shall touch the Crown upon her Majesty's head and kiss her Majesty's left cheek.

In like manner shall the Duke of Gloucester and the Duke of Kent severally do their homage. After which the Senior Peer of each degree (of the Dukes first by themselves, and so of the Marquesses, Earls, Viscounts, and Barons in that order) shall ascend the steps of the Throne and, having first removed his coronet, shall kneel before her Majesty and place his hands between the Queen's: and all the peers of his degree, having put off their coronets, shall kneel in their places and shall say with him:

I, N. Duke, or Earl, etc., of N.
do become your liege man of life and limb,
and of earthly worship;
and faith and truth I will bear unto you,
to live and die, against all manner of folks.
So help me God.

This done, the Senior Peer shall rise, and, all the Peers of his degree rising also, he shall touch the Crown upon her Majesty's head, as promising by that ceremony for himself and his Order to be ever ready to support it with all their power; and then shall he kiss the Queen's right hand.

At the same time the choir shall sing these anthems, or some of them:

Rejoice in the Lord alway,
and again I say, rejoice.
Let your moderation be known unto all men:
the Lord is even at hand.
Be careful for nothing:
but in all prayer and supplication, let your petitions be manifest unto God, with giving of thanks.
And the peace of God, which passeth all understanding,
keep your hearts and minds through Christ Jesu.
John Redford.

O clap your hands together, all ye people:
O sing unto God with the voice of melody.
For the Lord is high and to be feared:
he is the great King of all the earth.
He shall subdue the people under us:
and the nations under our feet.
He shall choose out an heritage for us:
even the worship of Jacob, whom he loved.
Orlando Gibbons.

I will not leave you comfortless. Alleluia.
I will go away and come again to you. Alleluia.
And your heart shall rejoice. Alleluia.
William Byrd.

O Lord our Governor:
how excellent is thy Name in all the world.

Behold, O God our defender:
and look upon the face of thine Anointed.
O hold thou up her goings in thy paths:
that her footsteps slip not.
Grant the Queen a long life:
and make her glad with the joy of thy countenance.
Save Lord and hear us O King of heaven:
when we call upon thee. Amen.
Healey Willan.

Thou wilt keep him in perfect peace,
whose mind is stayed on thee.
The darkness is no darkness with thee, but the night is as clear as day:
the darkness and the light are to thee both alike.
God is light,
and in him is no darkness at all.
O let my soul live,
and it shall praise thee.
For thine is the kingdom, the power and the glory,
for evermore.
Thou wilt keep him in perfect peace,
whose mind is stayed on thee.
Samuel Sebastian Wesley.

When the Homage is ended, the drums shall beat, and the trumpets sound, and all the people shout, crying out:

God save Queen ELIZABETH.

Long live Queen ELIZABETH.

May the Queen live forever

Then shall the Archbishop leave the Queen in her Throne and go to the Altar.

The Communion

Then shall the organ play and the people shall with one voice sing this hymn:

All people that on earth do dwell,
Sing to the Lord with cheerful voice;
Him serve with fear, his praise forth tell,

Come ye before him, and rejoice.

The Lord, ye know, is God indeed,
Without our aid he did us make;
We are his folk, he doth us feed,
And for his sheep he doth us take.

O enter then his gates with praise,
Approach with joy his courts unto;
Praise, laud, and bless his name always,
For it is seemly so to do.

For why? the Lord our God is good:
His mercy is for ever sure;
His truth at all times firmly stood,
And shall from age to age endure.

To Father, Son, and Holy Ghost,
The God whom heaven and earth adore,
From men and from the Angel-host
Be praise and glory evermore. Amen.

In the mean while the Queen shall descend from her Throne, supported and attended as before, and go to the steps of the Altar, where, delivering her Crown and her Sceptre and Rod to the Lord Great Chamberlain or other appointed Officers to hold, she shall kneel down.

The hymn ended and the people kneeling, first the Queen shall offer Bread and Wine for the Communion, which being brought out of Saint Edward's Chapel, and delivered into her hands (the Bread upon the Paten by the Bishop that read the Epistle, and the Wine in the Chalice by the Bishop that read the Gospel), shall be received from the Queen by the Archbishop, and reverently placed upon the Altar, and decently covered with a fair linen cloth, the Archbishop first saying this prayer:

Bless, O Lord, we beseech thee, these thy gifts,
and sanctify them unto this holy use,
that by them we may be made partakers of the Body and Blood
of thine only-begotten Son Jesus Christ,
and fed unto everlasting life of soul and body:
And that thy servant Queen ELIZABETH
may be enabled to the discharge of her weighty office,

whereunto of thy great goodness thou hast called and appointed her.
Grant this, O Lord, for Jesus Christ's sake,
our only Mediator and Advocate. Amen.

Then the Queen, kneeling as before, shall make her Oblation, offering a
Pall or Altar-cloth delivered by the Groom of the Robes to the Lord Great
Chamberlain, and by him, kneeling, to her Majesty, and an Ingot or Wedge of
Gold of a pound weight, which the Treasurer of the Household shall deliver
to the Lord Great Chamberlain, and he to her Majesty; and the Archbishop
coming to her, shall receive and place them upon the Altar.

Then shall the Queen go to her faldstool, set before the Altar between the steps
and King Edward's Chair, and the Duke of Edinburgh, coming to his faldstool
set beside the Queen's shall take off his coronet. Then shall they kneel down
together, and the Archbishop shall say this prayer:

Almighty God, the fountain of all goodness:
give ear, we beseech thee, to our prayers,
and multiply thy blessings upon this thy servant PHILIP
who with all humble devotion offers himself
for thy service in the dignity to which thou hast called him.
Defend him from all dangers, ghostly and bodily;
make him a great example of virtue and godliness,
and a blessing to the Queen and to her Peoples;
through Jesus Christ our Lord,
who liveth and reigneth with thee, O Father,
in the unity of the Holy Spirit,
one God, world without end. Amen.

Then shall the Archbishop bless the Duke, saying:

Almighty God,
to whom belongeth all power and dignity,
prosper you in your honour
and grant you therein long to continue,
fearing him always,
and always doing such things as please him,
through Jesus Christ our Lord. Amen.

Then the Archbishop, returning to the Altar, shall say:

Let us pray for the whole state of Christ's Church militant here in earth.

Almighty and ever living God, who by thy holy Apostle hast taught us to make prayers, and supplications, and to give thanks for all men: we humbly beseech thee most mercifully to accept these oblations, and to receive these our prayers which we offer unto thy Divine Majesty; beseeching thee to inspire continually the universal Church with the spirit of truth, unity, and concord: And grant, that all they that do confess thy holy Name may agree in the truth of thy holy Word, and live in unity and godly love.

We beseech thee also to save and defend all Christian Kings, Princes and Governors; and specially thy servant ELIZABETH our Queen; that under her we may be godly and quietly governed; and grant unto her whole Council, and to all that are put in authority under her, that they may truly and indifferently minister justice, to the punishment of wickedness and vice, and to the maintenance of thy true religion, and virtue.

Give grace, O heavenly Father, to all Bishops and Curates, that they may, both by their life and doctrine, set forth thy true and lively Word, and rightly and duly administer thy holy Sacraments; and to all thy people give thy heavenly grace; and specially to this congregation here present; that, with meek heart and due reverence, they may hear, and receive thy holy Word; truly serving thee in holiness and righteousness all the days of their life.

And we most humbly beseech thee of thy goodness, O Lord, to comfort and succour all them, who, in this transitory life, are in trouble, sorrow, need, sickness, or any other adversity.

And we also bless thy holy Name for all thy servants departed this life in thy faith and fear; beseeching thee to give us grace so to follow their good examples, that with them we may be partakers of thy heavenly kingdom:

Grant this, O Father, for Jesus Christ's sake, our only Mediator and Advocate. Amen.

The Exhortation.

Ye that do truly and earnestly repent you of your sins, and are in love and charity with your neighbours, and intend to lead a new life, following the commandments of God, and walking from henceforth in his holy ways; Draw near with faith, and take this holy Sacrament to your comfort; and make your humble confession to Almighty God, meekly kneeling upon your knees.

The General Confession.

Almighty God,
Father of our Lord Jesus Christ,
Maker of all things, Judge of all men;
We acknowledge and bewail our manifold sins and wickedness,
Which we, from time to time, most grievously have committed,
By thought, word, and deed,
Against thy Divine Majesty,
Provoking most justly thy wrath and indignation against us.
We do earnestly repent,
And are heartily sorry for these our misdoings;
The remembrance of them is grievous unto us;
The burden of them is intolerable.
Have mercy upon us,
Have mercy upon us, most merciful Father;
For thy Son our Lord Jesus Christ's sake,
Forgive us all that is past;
And grant that we may ever hereafter
Serve and please thee in newness of life,
To the honour and glory of thy Name;
Through Jesus Christ our Lord. Amen.

The Absolution.

Almighty God, our heavenly Father,
who of his great mercy
hath promised forgiveness of sins
to all them that with hearty repentance and true faith turn unto him;
Have mercy upon you;
pardon and deliver you from all your sins;
confirm and strengthen you in all goodness;
and bring you to everlasting life;
through Jesus Christ our Lord. Amen.

Then shall the Archbishop say:

Hear what comfortable words our Saviour Christ saith unto all that truly turn to him.

Come unto me, all that travail and are heavy laden,
and I will refresh you.
Matthew 11, 28.
So God loved the world, that he gave his only-begotten Son,
to the end that all that believe in him should not perish,
but have everlasting life.
John 3, 16.

Here also what Saint Paul saith.
This is a true saying, and worthy of all men to be received,
that Christ Jesus came into the world to save sinners.
I Timothy 1, 15.

Here also what Saint John saith.
If any man sin, we have an Advocate with the Father,
Jesus Christ the righteous;
and he is the propitiation for our sins.
1 John 2, 1.

After which the Archbishop shall proceed, saying:

Lift up your hearts.
Answer We lift them up unto the Lord.
Archbishop Let us give thanks unto our Lord God.
Answer It is meet and right so to do.

Then shall the Archbishop turn to the Lord's Table, and say:

It is very meet, right, and our bounden duty,
that we should at all times, and in all places,
give thanks unto thee,
O Lord, Holy Father,
Almighty, Everlasting God:

Who hast at this time consecrated thy servant
ELIZABETH to be our Queen,
that by the anointing of thy grace she may be
the Defender of thy Faith
and the Protector of thy Church and People.

Therefore with Angels and Archangels,
and with all the company of heaven,

we laud and magnify thy glorious Name;
evermore praising thee, and saying:
Holy, holy, holy, Lord God of Hosts,
heaven and earth are full of thy glory.
Glory be to thee, O Lord most high. Amen.

The Prayer of Humble Access:

We do not presume
to come to this thy Table, O merciful Lord,
trusting in our own righteousness,
but in thy manifold and great mercies.
We are not worthy
so much as to gather up the crumbs under thy Table.
But thou art the same Lord,
whose property is always to have mercy.
Grant us therefore, gracious Lord,
so to eat the flesh of thy dear Son Jesus Christ,
and to drink his blood,
that our sinful bodies may be made clean by his body,
and our souls washed through his most precious blood,
and that we may evermore dwell in him, and he in us. Amen.

The Prayer of Consecration:

Almighty God, our heavenly Father,
who of thy tender mercy
didst give thine only Son Jesus Christ
to suffer death upon the cross for our redemption;
who made there
(by his one oblation of himself once offered)
a full, perfect, and sufficient sacrifice, oblation, and satisfaction,
for the sins of the whole world;
and did institute,
and in his holy Gospel command us to continue,
a perpetual memory of that his precious death,
until his coming again;

Hear us, O merciful Father,
we most humbly beseech thee;
and grant that we, receiving these thy creatures of bread and wine,
according to thy Son our Saviour Jesus Christ's holy institution,

in remembrance of his death and passion,
may be partakers of his most blessed Body and Blood:
Who in the same night that he was betrayed,
Here the Archbishop is to take the Paten into his hands:
took Bread; and, when he had given thanks,
And here to break the Bread:
he brake it, and gave it to his disciples, saying,
Take, eat,
And here to lay his hand upon the Bread:
this is my Body, which is given for you:
Do this in remembrance of me.

Likewise, after supper,
Here he is to take the Cup into his hand:
he took the Cup;
and when he had given thanks,
he gave it to them, saying,
Drink ye all of this;
for this
And here to lay his hand upon the Cup.
is my Blood of the New Testament,
which is shed for you and for many
for the remission of sins:

Do this, as oft as ye shall drink it,
in remembrance of me. Amen.

When the Archbishops, and the Dean of Westminster, with the Bishops
Assistant (namely, those who carried the Bible, Paten and Chalice in the
Procession), have communicated in both kinds, the Queen with the Duke of
Edinburgh shall advance to the steps of the Altar and, both kneeling down, the
Archbishop shall administer the Bread, and the Dean of Westminster the Cup,
to them. And in the meantime the choir shall sing:

O taste, and see, how gracious the Lord is:
blessed is the man that trusteth in him.
Psalm 34, 8.

At the delivery of the Bread shall be said:
The Body of our Lord Jesus Christ, which was given for thee,
preserve thy body and soul unto everlasting life.
Take and eat this in remembrance that Christ died for thee,

and feed on him in thy heart by faith, with thanksgiving.

At the delivery of the Cup:
The Blood of our Lord Jesus Christ, which was shed for thee,
preserve thy body and soul unto everlasting life.
Drink this in remembrance that Christ's Blood was shed for thee,
and be thankful.

After which the Queen and the Duke of Edinburgh shall return to their
faldstools; and the Archbishop shall go on to the Post-Communion, he and all
the people saying:

Our Father, which art in heaven,
Hallowed be thy Name.
Thy kingdom come.
Thy will be done
in earth, as it is in heaven.
Give us this day our daily bread.
And forgive us our trespasses,
As we forgive them that trespass against us.
And lead us not into temptation;
But deliver us from evil:
For thine is the kingdom,
The power, and the glory,
For ever and ever. Amen.

And after shall be said as followeth:

O Lord and heavenly Father,
we thy humble servants
entirely desire thy fatherly goodness
mercifully to accept this our sacrifice of praise and thanksgiving;
most humbly beseeching thee to grant, that
by the merits and death of thy Son Jesus Christ,
and through faith in his blood,
we, and all thy whole Church,
may obtain remission of our sins,
and all other benefits of his passion.
And here we offer and present unto thee, O Lord,
ourselves, our souls and bodies,
to be a reasonable, holy, and lively sacrifice unto thee;
humbly beseeching thee, that all we,

who are partakers of this holy Communion,
may be fulfilled with thy grace and heavenly benediction.
And although we be unworthy, through our manifold sins,
to offer unto thee any sacrifice,
yet we beseech thee
to accept this our bounden duty and service;
not weighing our merits, but pardoning our offences,
through Jesus Christ our Lord;
by whom, and with whom,
in the unity of the Holy Ghost,
all honour and glory be unto thee,
O Father Almighty, world without end. Amen.

Then, all the people standing, the Queen shall rise and, receiving again her Crown and taking the Sceptre and Rod into her hands, shall repair to her Throne; and the Duke, putting on his coronet, shall return to his place.

Then shall be sung:
Glory be to God on high,
and in earth peace, good will towards men.
We praise thee, we bless thee,
we worship thee, we glorify thee,
we give thanks to thee for thy great glory,
O Lord God, heavenly King,
God the Father Almighty.

O Lord, the only-begotten Son, Jesus Christ;
O Lord God, Lamb of God, Son of the Father,
that takest away the sins of the world,
have mercy upon us.

Thou that takest away the sins of the world,
have mercy upon us.
Thou that takest away the sins of the world,
receive our prayer.
Thou that sittest at the right hand of God the Father,
have mercy upon us.
For thou only art holy;
thou only art the Lord;
thou only, O Christ,
with the Holy Ghost,
art most high

in the glory of God the Father. Amen.

Then, the people kneeling, the Archbishop shall say:
Prevent us, O Lord, in all our doings
with thy most gracious favour,
and further us with thy continual help;
that in all our works begun, continued, and ended in thee,
we may glorify thy holy Name,
and finally by thy mercy obtain everlasting life;
through Jesus Christ our Lord. Amen.

The peace of God, which passeth all understanding,
keep your hearts and minds in the knowledge and love of God,
and of his Son Jesus Christ our Lord;
and the blessing of God Almighty,
the Father, the Son, and the Holy Ghost,
be amongst you, and remain with you always. Amen.

XVI.

The solemnity of the Queen's Coronation being thus ended, the people shall
stand, and the choir shall sing:

Te Deum Laudamus

We praise thee, O God:
we acknowledge thee to be the Lord.
All the earth doth worship thee:
the Father everlasting.
To thee all Angels cry aloud:
the heavens and all the powers therein.
To thee Cherubim and Seraphim:
continually do cry,
Holy, Holy, Holy:
Lord God of Sabaoth;
Heaven and earth are full of the Majesty:
of thy Glory.
The glorious company of the Apostles:
praise thee.
The goodly fellowship of the Prophets:
praise thee.
The noble army of Martyrs:

praise thee.
The holy Church throughout all the world:
doth acknowledge thee;
The Father:
of an infinite majesty;
Thine honourable, true:
and only Son;
Also the Holy Ghost:
the Comforter.
Thou art the King of Glory:
O Christ.
Thou art the everlasting Son:
of the Father.
When thou tookest upon thee to deliver man:
thou didst not abhor the Virgin's womb.
When thou hadst overcome the sharpness of death:
thou didst open the kingdom of heaven to all believers.
Thou sittest at the right hand of God:
in the glory of the Father.
We believe that thou shalt come:
to be our Judge.
We therefore pray thee, help thy servants:
whom thou hast redeemed with thy precious blood.
Make them to be numbered with thy Saints:
in glory everlasting.
O Lord, save thy people:
and bless thine heritage.
Govern them:
and lift them up for ever.
Day by day:
we magnify thee;
And we worship thy Name:
ever world without end.
Vouchsafe, O Lord:
to keep us this day without sin.
O Lord, have mercy upon us:
have mercy upon us.
O Lord, let thy mercy lighten upon us:
as our trust is in thee.
O Lord, in thee have I trusted:
let me never be confounded.

The Recess

In the meantime, the Queen, supported as before, the four swords being carried before her, shall descend from her Throne, crowned and carrying the Sceptre and the Rod in her hands, and shall go into the Area eastward of the Theatre; and, the Archbishop going before her, she shall pass on through the door on the south side of the Altar into Saint Edward's Chapel; and after her shall follow the Groom of the Robes, the Lord Great Chamberlain and the Lords that carried the Regalia in the procession (the Dean of Westminster delivering the Orb, the Spurs and St Edward's Staff to the Bearers of them as they pass the Altar); and lastly shall go in the Dean.

And, the Te Deum ended, the people may be seated until the Queen comes again from the Chapel.

The Queen, being come into the Chapel, shall deliver to the Archbishop, being at the Altar there, the Sceptre and the Rod to be laid upon the Altar: and the Archbishop shall receive the Queen's Crown and lay it upon the Altar also. Then, assisted by the Mistress of the Robes, and attended by the Lord Great Chamberlain and the Groom of the Robes, the Queen shall be disrobed of the Robe Royal and arrayed in her Robe of purple velvet.

Meanwhile the Dean of Westminster shall lay upon the Altar the Orb, the Spurs and St Edward's Staff, having received them from the Bearers of them, who shall then (preceded by the Bearers of the Four Swords) withdraw from the Chapel by the same door on the south side and take the places assigned to them in the procession.

The Queen being ready, and wearing her Imperial Crown, shall receive the Sceptre with the Cross into her right hand and into her left hand the Orb from the Archbishop, who, having delivered them, shall withdraw from the Chapel and take his place in the procession: and the Lord Great Chamberlain shall do likewise.

Then her Majesty, supported and attended as before, shall leave the Chapel by the same door on the south side and shall proceed in state through the choir and the nave to the west door of the Church, wearing her Crown and bearing in her right hand the Sceptre and in her left hand the Orb.

And as the Queen proceeds from the Chapel, there shall be sung by all assembled the National Anthem.

End of Ceremony

Our society is influenced by the fraternities and the brotherhoods with the Queen of England being at the head of the 'Order of the Garter' a high ranking Masonic order.

When Masons reach the third degree they can chose between the York rite and Scottish rite, the Scottish rite of freemasonry deals with all things Egyptian and the word Mason derives from Ma'son, the mother son, which is Sirius A, associated with the Egyptian Goddess Isis (The Blazing Star as it known in Masonic circles).

It is believed to be the mother of our solar sun and the original Mary and Jesus in reality is is Isis and Horus. Mother Mary is the Christianised version of this Egyptian Goddess. Isis is also associated astronomically with the Moon, especially the New Moon, which appears as the waters of the Nile rise and in turn gives rise to the land to become fertile enabling crops and vegetation to grow.

The Moon takes the same transit as the Sun and its transit makes an East to West arch as does the sun, this is a Moon-arch from where we get the word Monarch!

All that is Royal is really Egyptian in origin even the Royal crown which is a physical personification of the Crown chakra. The Queen's face is on all Bank of England monetary notes and again this is the Egyptian principle marking the power of that individual.

Our linearage comes from a place of wonder, a place of deep esoteric knowledge that has been hidden by initiations and public symbology that masks a language for those select few to speak and that doesn't include the rest of the population who are fed an exoteric version of the truth to keep our minds unliberated; to keep us milling the machines and waking the treadmills.

SOME EGYPTIAN SYMBOLS IN MODERN SOCIETY: (There are a multitude of others):

It is said that we see at least 1000 hidden symbols each day; but because it is a hidden language of the initiates. Within our mind they go unnoticed by us, however not so much so in the sub-conscious mind (sub-conscious meaning below awareness) it is much different there; it is impactful.

It is true that other cultures have influence such as Babylon and the London Mayors office is based on the tower of Babel. As such the London MI6 Building is built in Babylonian style building; the Ziggurat. The building is nick-named 'Babylon on the Thames'. But the main influence, as you will see, is Egypt when we also look into architecture and alike. We also see these references in corporate logos and many famous and household brand names.

(Left: Big Ben, London, UK. Right: The American Dollar bill with pyramid)

Above is Big Ben at the London Houses of Parliament, the centre of UK government. Big Ben is a nick name that derives from the Benbenet stone which is the Pyramid capstone and above we also see the American dollar with the Pyramid and 'All Seeing Eye' (enlightenment at the top of the apex which I go into later) The word Parliament derives from Parler-Ment meaning to speak your mind.

The portcullis emblem on some English coins and also on the seats of the House of Commons is the 'Hoshen' the breast plate of the serpent priests.

The river Thames in London (Thames deriving from Tamas = Dark river) was formerly called Isis, it is still; even today; called Isis in parts of Oxfordshire. When you walk along the Thames you see the likes of Egyptian statues, Lions and Cleopatra's needle (obelisk) but many just see it at face value as nice décor but it has a much deeper and wider symbology out of the wavelength of most people's antennae's. Even the Cenotaph in central London, the scene of Remembrance Day parades attended by Royalty and Government; is an obelisk.

(Pyramid on top of Canary Wharf, the business centre in London's East End)

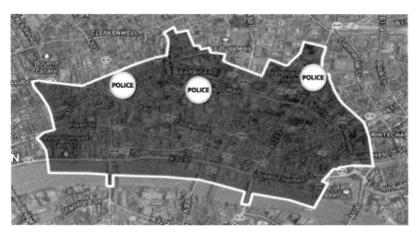

(City of London Police Stations mapping the Orion's Belt Constellation)

Even the City of London Police; police stations (UK); are mapped out in the shape of the 3 stars of Orion's belt. The City of London has a moto of '' Domine Dirige Nos which means O Lord Direct us... You will find out the meaning of Lord later on.

(St George's Flag of England)

Flag of St George (UK) which indicates the merging of lower (Red) and Upper (White) Egypt and the American dollar sign revealed as Isis, the Egyptian Goddess. George derives from Djeudje (Set/Sunset) and Apophis (Darkness who fought the Sun; hence sunset; each night) is the dragon, in Egyptian they call this Westing, meaning to die. This is English legend of George and the Dragon. Good old English pub names such as the most popular pub name; the 'Red Lion'; is symbolic of the Pharaohs of Lower Egypt. The Red, white and blue of many national flags is Egyptian Royalty merging the two lands.

(The Mini Logo - a symbol of RA)

Corporate logos also contain Egyptian symbology too such as Mini, the cerebellum (Little Brain) and the wings, the Lateral Hemispheres and the Black Dot, the Aten (again I will detail this later). But nevertheless it is all Egyptian symbology in plain sight; seen each and every day by thousands of unaware people.

(The Oval Office at the Presidential White House – Oval is the shape of the Pituitary Gland associated with motherhood; Isis)

(The American Dollar sign concealing the Egyptian Goddess)

Even the American currency with its dollar sign has Isis connotations as you will see in the image opposite, below center.

(Obelisk in Washington DC)

Memphis the former Egyptian capital means 'White Walls' no coincidence. And the Washington Obelisk (Penis of Egyptian God Osiris) and the Dome shaped building again representing motherhood. The Washington DC obelisk was erected at the exact time that Sirius passed over the Sun. The celebration of mother's day is also Isis ritual, Magna Mater, great mother and likewise we are celebrating the solar Sun in relation to Father's day, celebrating our father on 21st June (UK) which is the date of the start of the Summer Solstice.

The founding fathers signed the declaration of Independence on 4th July which is when Sirius 'A' (cosmic egg - Isis) is furthest away from our Sun, in its Binary and out of sight which they wanted to commemorate this into American history. The declaration was signed in Philadelphia which is significant because Philae in Egypt is where the Temple of Isis stands and Delphi (Delphos) means Womb which relates to Isis as the mother Goddess, also with Pituitary Gland implications. The American emblem, the Eagle, is also an Egyptian symbol (Am-Erica = Eternal rule of the Eagle).

The Sun-Sirius binary is also relevant in the Hopi-Indian Red & Blue star Kachina prophesy. On the star colour chart (the Doppler effect), which is coloured depending on such things as vibration and light reflection; Sirius is Red going away from the Sun and blue on its way back.

(Lion and Unicorn Royal Crest)

The Royal Crest above, the Unicorn (Third Eye energy spiral represented by the Horn) and the Lion representing the Sun (Roar = Or-RA, Golden Sun, God energy) are in unison together and a third eye activation symbol, the unicorn's chain is broken and its inner potential is released). In King Arthur; Arthurian legend; this was what was meant by the sword Excalibur being removed from the stone by the worthy. The Stone is the Foundation stone which is a name for the Pineal gland, the sword represents impenetrable knowledge and Excalibur derives from Ex- Calce- Liberatus meaning 'Liberated from the stone' in Latin. In other words; Only the worthy, the chosen can extract the knowledge from the Pineal gland.

When we eat a hotdog, the American way, we are engaged in an Egyptian ritual of dog sacrifice to Sirius and our solar sun to appease the heat of the summer sun a period called dog days.

(The Statue Of Liberty (Isis), New York)

The Statue of Liberty in New York is really Isis (or Semiramis in Babylonian culture holding onto the flame, Nimrod, Babylonian Sun-God). Her crown are the Sun's rays/corona. Liberty faces Paris and the Champs-Elysees meaning 'City of Light' close to the Arc De Triomphe, the arc of the Sun. The Parisian street map; leading to the Arc De Triomphe; represent the Sun's rays when seen from above. The Louver gallery is also a giant glass pyramid. The centre of Paris itself is home to a large obelisk.

And even popular sporting events are not immune as thousands cheer in ignorance, here's the super-bowl 2012; full of Osirian symbology.

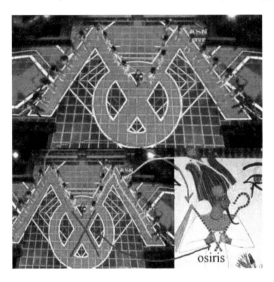

(The Symbology of 2012's Super Bowl - Osiris)

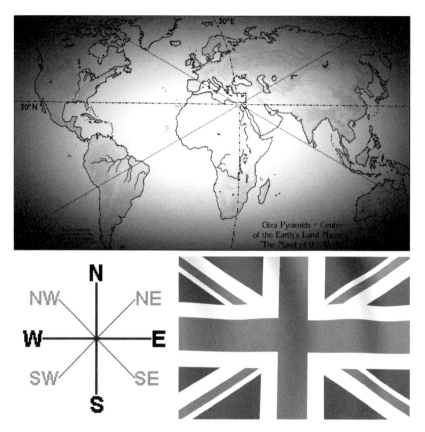

(The compass points on a world map illustrate the exact location of Giza in Egypt, which can be seen here at the centre of the line formation. When we see the Union Jack, the flag of the UK, the same shape can be seen, the centre is again the location of Giza. The red, white and blue colours indicates the blue of royalty and the red and white indicates upper and lower Egypt combined.)

The examples are totally endless and I could have filled this book with the symbols that I personally see each day alone.

Egypt penetrates the heart of government and Royalty because it is all connected by a linear genetic line. It is more influential than any other culture and its connection still remains in our society even through to our leaders and Royalty and through our spiritual nature that has far greater potential than it is being allowed to know by those holding on to a deeper esoteric knowledge that could enlighten the world. But for those who know, they want to keep us from ever knowing so that they can keep their advantage over us.

5

THE GENESIS - THE GENE OF ISIS

Religion, the Bible and its globally famous characters, were a creation of man. These teachings have many levels of meaning that tell a story and dependent upon your level of understanding that story can be totally different from one person to the next. The masses attend Church every Sunday and listen to historical sermons delivered in now vanished times by the Messiah and by others reportedly documented many hundreds of years after the event.

They tell of physical beings such as Christ, Moses, Mother Mary, Mary Magdalene, Noah and many others who walked the Earth as people. They tell of miracles and justice and they tell of our need for reliance of these people to save us and bring us salvation for our sins. But what if a deeper truth is being hidden from us, a truth that these characters were not actually real people?

Instead, what if the stories that have become the most read and loved paragraphs and parables the world has ever seen are really a cover-up for something much more beautiful, much more divine and sacred, that being the Deity, Deit, which means 'self'?

The Egyptians knew all about the self, which you will read in later chapters, they left this knowledge for us to find and decipher, but that knowledge has been kept from us by those who wish to keep us subservient and obedient to a system devised to keep us within it and reliant upon an outside source, and therefore denying ourselves. The whole system we call religion is esoterically based upon this fact, based upon humanity being God-like potential. The stories given to us are really referring to the stars, astronomy and the genetics of the human body which are connected by a mystical marriage called 'Medical Astronomy'.

The solar sun's photons connect to human DNA by virtue of coded messages and frequencies; it is in itself another language of the genetic kind. Jesus speaks to us genetically through the Sermon on the Mount; our holy place, our mind.

All the famous characters of such religious books, such as the Bible, can be attributed to the workings of space and the human body. The version of events given to us as a population; a portrayal of what was meant to have happened all those centuries ago; are really the brilliant genetic system of our physical incarnation.

Once this is known then we can as a race begin to transcend to our rightful place. Religion as we know it also has its origins in Egypt. But before I go into Egypt and its advanced knowledge, let's first analyse the famous biblical characters and show you how they are in fact not real people; but instead a great and hidden metaphor; an allegory, a story with a hidden meaning.

THE GENESIS:

In the Beginning Was The Word...

The Bible states that 'In the beginning was the word', but what was the word? Human DNA has 4 nucleotides namely Adenine, Thymine, Guanine and Cytosine and their letters have 64 combinations, they are a language, an alphabet (64 Keys of Enoch is also referring to this).

In basic Gemetria which is the numerical value of words/letters the number 64 is God. Therefore the statement "In the Beginning was the word and the word was with God" is really talking about human DNA, the building blocks of life, where life started, programmed to become a manifestation, to grow in sequences of 8 as it creates through the Genesis pattern until we reach the 64 tetrahedron grid, full development. We demonstrate a miniature cosmos as life starts within our small universe; the human body.

ADAM & EVE:

Where It All Started

Adam and Eve were the first people to inhabit the world; according to the bible and its divisions of the Hebrew Scriptures. Eve was created from the rib of Adam and they lived peacefully together in the Garden of Eden, Eden meaning Paradise. We all come from Adam which is really referring to the atom. But Eve was tempted by the serpent to eat the forbidden fruit from the tree of knowledge, good and evil.

The apple is associated with knowledge; a revelatory state; revealing something unknown. It is an allusion; a figure of speech, in which one refers covertly or indirectly to an object or circumstance from an external context. It is left to the audience to make the connection. In other words it has a hidden meaning; knowledge hidden from the masses but not the select few, this knowledge is what they wish to keep to themselves; stated directly or in this case indirectly by its author in the same vein as political double speak, saying one thing but actually meaning something else. There is effectively two languages being spoken in parallel. It is an allegory, a story with a hidden meaning and it is for us to decipher the clues.

But did the story of Adam and Eve really happen?

In the physical sense no. Adam is referring again to the universal and human make-up; the atom. The creation of Eve from Adam is talking about ionic bonding, the electron being passed between atoms; the electron is a current of negative charge which is why Eve is seen as a negative influence on Adam. From Adam (atom) we get Eve in the form of ionic bonding, the electron exchange between atoms. Adam means Man and Eve means Life which is PI-Electron Density in relation to DNA synthesis, the repair and duplication of cells which is required for them to live in the chaotic environment of our body.

The word body in Germanic was originally Bodig/Leib meaning 'life', as does the word and name Eve. The feminine principle is magnetic force which is a negative current. Many of the world religions devalue women and the feminine polarity and this is scientifically why. This is symbolized by head and face coverings in the many world religions, the concealment of shame. The fig leaf is also symbolic of covering shame. Nakedness is symbolic of the truth, or what is revealed.

In essence we have Atom and Eve, inside our body; the spine is the tree of life with all its nerves which are its branches on the tree. The serpent is our Kundalini energy (meaning coiled) that travels up the spine (Jacobs Ladder) entwining itself around the bark (33 steps of the spinal column or the 33 degrees of freemasonry) up to the top where we find the forbidden fruit.

The forbidden fruit is the pineal gland which is named after the pine-cone which it resembles and that contains the pine-nut (fruit with a hard shell) which is the forbidden fruit, knowledge from our third eye chakra, the 'all seeing eye' which again has Egyptian connotations that I will detail later. To forbid also means to deny entry into a place; in this case the place of knowledge. In other words; you are forbidden from entering that place of knowing, what they know; the knowledge that they retain for themselves and closely guard in the best place possible, right in front of our face.

It has been stated that Eden is located by the 4 rivers and various scholars have attempted to find the Earthly physical land where Eden was located. However they will not find it. They will not find it because again it is within the body; the 4 rivers are our body fluids networks. Eden's garden; as stated; is the human body: Here are the 4 rivers in question and this is what they correspond to:

- PISHON, a stream of urine…

- HIDIKEL, which means blood…

- GIHON, derived from the verb meaning "to gush forth", and is the intestinal tract…

- EUPHRATES, meaning good water, is the nerve fluid…

From the Adam/atom we get another biblical story of the 'Holy Trinity'. This is again the 3 component parts of the atom. The Neutron is the father; the Proton is the son and the Electron is the Holy Ghost/Spirit. When electrons become ionized and excited they give off a cloud which is called an 'Electron Cloud' this bares striking similarity to a ghost, this is the Holy Ghost or Holy Spirit. A spirit is the non-decaying spin of the electron that can enter different realms by transiting between magnetic field lines.

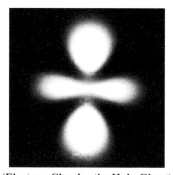

(Electron Cloud = the Holy Ghost)

This story, as with the others I will now detail, is not talking about physical people, it is referring to our greatness within; the 'Human Body'.

Jesus Was Not A Man – So Who/What Was He?
(The Christ)

In my book 'The Secret of Christ – The Christos Code' I go deep into the astronomical meanings of religions et al. I am about to briefly mention a little astronomy now to enhance a point, however since this book is more about 'Genetic Consciousness' it will revert back to the human body, albeit the universe and the human body are connected by 'Medical Astronomy' and are one of the same. They are simply just a microcosmic and macrocosmic version of each other.

Jesus was the anointed one and anointed means to oil, he is the messiah, the anticipated saviour. When people speak of and refer to Jesus many believe in a physical man who walked the Middle East.

The character Jesus the man is a story that is referring to each of us, it is talking about ourselves; we are all the Christ, each and every one of us and here's how.

Imagine ancient man struggling for survival on planet Earth, the dark of night looms, a time when he was vulnerable and open to be hunted by larger carnivores, unable to effectively see his surroundings; Seeking shelter and warmth and protection. Then after he spotted the planet Venus he had the promise of the Sun as he knows that the Sun rises second in the sky after the morning star.

This is the second coming (Of Christ).

Now the world is lit, man can see; the Sun is the saviour, it says "I am the light of the world", "Every eye shall see him" (Jesus quotes) although this not necessarily referring entirely to the physical eyes. The Sun in Hebrew is called Yes/Jes which is where we get the names Yeshua and Jesus and in the Chaldean language the Sun is called Chris (as in Christ).

When we nod our heads and say 'yes' we are symbolising Sun rise and Sun set. In ancient days the word Son and Sun were the same word, deriving from the German word Sonne; separated by early Christians to create a division to hide the true nature and meaning of this golden globe in the sky.

Astronomically Jesus is a metaphor for the solar sun and the life of Jesus is the Sun's transit through the 12 signs of the zodiac or in biblical terminology the 12 disciples who tell his story; the celestial narrative detailing the life of the Sun. But in bodily terms the 12 disciples are the 12 Cranial nerves that live around the Christ in his everyday life and existence. They are as follows:

CRANIAL NERVE: Major Functions: The 12 Disciples of the Christ:

I - Olfactory smell

II - Optic vision

III - Oculomotor eyelid and eyeball movement

IV - Trochlear innervates superior oblique turns eye downward and laterally

V - Trigeminal chewing, face & mouth touch & pain

VI - Abducens turns eye laterally

VII - Facial controls most facial expressions, secretion of tears & saliva taste

VIII - Vestibulocochlear(auditory) hearing, equilibrium, sensation

IX - Glossopharyngeal taste, senses, carotid blood pressure

X - Vagus senses, aortic blood pressure, slows heart rate, stimulates digestive organs taste

XI - Spinal Accessory controls trapezius & sternocleidomastoid controls swallowing movements

XII - Hypoglossal controls tongue movements

NOW FOR SOME MORE ASTRONOMY:

On December 25th each year the Sun moves 1 degree north to begin its annual transit, after spending 3 days, namely the 22nd/23rd/24th December within the same degree of sky, not moving; hence the Sun was dead for 3 days before it rose again (that leads onto Easter). It was stated in the bible regarding Jesus that "he rose early on the first day of the week", that is referring to Sunday sunrise.

Such festivals as Easter also have sun connotations; such as the word contained within; namely East from Ost which means dawn, to become light. The sun rises over the equator, or in Judaic circles; the Passover, the sun passing over the equator itself, in Christianity this is the Sun/Son rise, when Jesus rose from the tomb.

On 25th December the Sun/Jesus is born by virtue of that 1 degree movement. This date may be quite important to many as they celebrate with gifts and enjoy family company each year, without knowing the astronomical relevance and origins of their efforts; it is Sun worship, the visible Sun and as I will go into later it is also worship of the hidden Sun, our own internal wisdom and divinity.

Our internal wisdom; our inner Christ; is relevant throughout this book and there are many references to our own personal divinity which is within us all.

Now back to the body!

In body universe terms; Jesus is the messiah; he is the anointed and anointed means to oil or to be oiled. To oil also means to impregnate which has other meanings other than the obvious to make pregnant, such as to lubricate, saturate or soak (for example pineal gland secretion/oil).

Our many bodily fluids carry the Christ solar seed/oil of Christ, that Mary (the Ida within the brain) was impregnated with eventually leading to a 'virgin birth'. Ida = um = womb - in other words saturated by oil.

The word seed means sperm and the male testicles also go through the stomach; more precisely, through the cluster of nerves called the celiac plexus, popularly known as the solar plexus; therefore our Christ (seed) was born in Bethlehem. The Solar plexus is called Bethlehem and the word Bethlehem literally means 'House of Bread' which also relates to a seed. Celiac (coeliac) means Belly. The solar plexus and cerebrum within the brain are connected by nerve filaments conveying messages (brain to brain). It also controls the instinctive mind.

A plexus is a network and in bodily terms it relates to nerve endings and alike. The Christ (or Christ seed) is crucified which also means to 'subdue ones appetites' and there we have celibacy, saving the seed and not wasting it. The seed travels through the optic chiasm which was given the name of the Crossing by the Greeks as it is formed in the shape of a cross; therefore the Christ seed is crucified on the cross. The crucified seed is retained in the body and used in various places including the higher chakras, heaven, upon crucifixion; as I will explain later on in this section.

LIVING IN SIN:

We are told that we are all living in Sin but that really means Sine (sin is an abbreviation of sine) which means the ratio of the side of a right angle. The symbol for 'inverse sine' is sin. Within the body there is what is called the 'transverse plane' that is the one passing horizontally through the body, at right angles to the sagittal and frontal planes and dividing the body into upper and lower portions; heaven and Earth. We are entities of two halves.

We were all born with original sin, we are living in our lower chakras, the lower part of the transverse plane, the lower density kingdom of Earth (lower chakras) our lower places. We are born in Gods image, The 'Geometry of Divinity' G.O.D.

Whereas the Kingdom of heaven is the higher chakras; leading to the God-state which we have not yet reached. Sin/sine in biblical terms is anything that separates us from God, the division of the body into two halves whereby we're living in the lower half is doing just that.

Jesus was crucified on the cross to save us from sin (see optic chiasm section) which takes us from the kingdom of Earth to the kingdom of heaven during the kundalini awakening process, raising us from the lower to the higher places saving us from the lower chakras caused as a result of sine/sin. And as a footnote my nationality is English and English means 'Man of Angles'.

Sarah, my wife, having read this chapter posed a very potent question to me, that being if the Christ seed is male sperm generated inside the male body then how can women become enlightened?

In addition to the unused sperm that would be used in the same internal fashion as in the male body the female have something else as a substitute germ, which is the "lunar germ". The Lunar germ originates in the pituitary body within the brain and follows a path by way of the fourth ventricle down the spine and into the reproductive organs which combines chemically to aid in the production of sperm.

If the germ is not lost in sexual activities it travels back up along the spinal cord and back into the brain where it combines with something known as the 'solar germ' (Christ seed). In each month, after puberty, the generative system produces one of these lunar germs in the pituitary body.

GOING BACK TO THE CRUCIFIXION

The now famous 5 wounds of 'Yahshuah' seen on the cross are the letters of his name in pentagrammation, the 5 letter divine name. Yahshuah is a form of the

Hebrew name Jesus. Penta means 5 and the Greek gramma meaning letters. We start as the tetragram, the 4 elements and then reach the pentagram, the fifth point of the star, the finished star (ether) with conscious awakening and the balance of the primal elements of Fire, Earth, Water and Air, the essential elements for life on the physical/material realm. We progress from the Earth state of 4 elements to the ether, the fifth element as we consciously ascend out of the physical/material realm.

This X shape crossing; the Optic Chiasm; is portrayed widely in Egyptian statues and hieroglyphs and is the symbol of the God Osiris, it means chamber of light. The Optic Chiasm is connected to the Pineal gland, the throne of God which is again another hidden clue of our inner enlightenment.

(X Shape crossing symbolism)

The Optic Chiasm is where the optic nerves partially cross below the Hypothalamus.

The Saviour literally means 'one who sows the seed' and Yeshua means Salvation! 1/10 of these fluids, from where we get the word and ritual of tithing (meaning 10th) is refined within the body and such practices as Celibacy derives from saving this seed; by not wasting the seed carrying fluids at ejaculation; thou salt not commit adultery, in other words you shall not waste the sacred seed; although this is not widely known, especially by priests.

In physical symbology some religions get a 10% donation of a person's salary and when in Church they pass around the tray for donations this is again symbolic of tithing, (salary derives from sal meaning salt).

The Thalamus, the Christ of our brain, is known as the RU (Gateway) and when we hear Jesus saying such quotes as this;

"Only through me will you reach the father" it is telling us that enlightenment gets activated and we reconnect to the father (ether) through Th(RU)gh him as our kundalini energy sparks cosmic connection. I go into this later in the Egypt section.

(The Priests Dog-Collar and attire is symbolic of this Jesus quote/statement)

The now famous gifts brought to Jesus by the 3 wise men, namely of Frankincense, myrrh and Gold is again referring to the Pineal Gland (Frankincense) Myrrh (Pituitary Gland) and Gold (Chemical Gold) the Thalamus, the 3 component parts of the endocrine system . The 3 wise men travelled by Camel, camel deriving from gamal meaning 'Path finder' and the story is one of looking for and finding enlightenment, locating the Christ seed.

Seminal Retention:

Higher consciousness and sexual sublimation (diverting sexual energy to the brain) are used for kundalini activation; this is the required balance of the two needed to achieve Kundalini awakening.

.
"When the desires are stirred, it runs downward, is directed outward, and creates children. If in the moment of release, it is not allowed to flow outward, but is led back by the energy of thought so that it penetrates the crucible of the Creative, and refreshes heart and body and nourishes them, that is also the backward-flowing method."- (Courtesy of Secret of the Golden Flower)

This is the exocrine system (exocrine meaning secrete outwards) that can be retained within for our endocrine system (secrete within) as part of the journey of our own Christ; the Christ within. The giving and receiving energies, masculine outward bursts and feminine inward bursts. "Because of me, man shall live forever", (seed of life).

Any semen which is not ejaculated is simply absorbed by the body to be reused by other cells. Human testis and brain share the highest similarity of gene expression patterns. Gonadotropin or Gonadotropin Hormones have a stimulating effect on the gonads and are secreted by the anterior Pituitary Gland (anterior meaning towards the front of the body). The hypothalamus secretes this hormone into the pituitary gland in the brain. The pituitary gland secretes this hormone after receiving a signal from the hypothalamus in a close synergy between the two. The story of the virgin birth is again referring to a bodily reproduction function and not physical people like we've been deliberately led to believe and have been wrongly informed.

The seed remains in the skull cavern (tomb/cerebellum) for 1 moon sign, the equivalent of 3 days; before it ascends to the pineal gland.

Our spinal fluids; which assist in the transit of the Seed; contain Sodium Chloride, salt, Sal, we are our own salvation and the word and name Yeshua means Salvation. It is all within us.

The Ida is connected to the Moon and the Pingala is connected to the Sun; the masculine and feminine counterparts; the energy flow of the left and right hemispheres of the brain and through the human body and there we have Mary and Joseph and the solar seed, the Christos, the Christ, the oiled/anointed seed carried in the fluid/flowing substance called semen, the seed collecting its oil. Together in this triad we have the Mother and father and the Christ child, Mary, Joseph and Jesus.

Christ was called the Good Shepherd and a good shepherd supplies all that is needed for his flock. Anatomically our Solar Plexus (house of bread) feeds our brain supplying all that it needs, one of the meanings of the word shepherd is 'feeder' and this is the relationship that our Solar Plexus and brain have together (solar plexus is our abdominal brain).

Therefore the Lord (Lord meaning 'giver of bread') is our shepherd; the place where the Christ seed grows; feeds the brain. It is all a metaphor for the workings of the human body. A sheep grazes on grass and grass is an analogy for flesh, our body.

The crown of thorns that was placed on the head of Jesus is symbolic and has an esoteric meaning. The crown of thorns has a correspondence with the crown star (or "chakra"), as well as to the brow star with the uplifting of the serpent power to the brow or crown and the repose (a state of mind) or cessation of the serpent power through which Supernal (sky) or Messianic Consciousness dawns, a place where the physical meets the metaphysical at the point of awakening.

The crown of thorns is also taken to represent the need to bring mental consciousness into cessation (end/cease), in other words symbolically to be awakened beyond the physical mind (physical brain).

THE OPPOSITES:

The Pingala is Red and the Ida is blue, fire and water; dualistic opposites. It is again the wondrous workings of our bodies. Pingala = At = Ptah = Father and Joseph was the father of Jesus.

The Egyptian goddess of balance was Ma'at which means Mother and father, a masculine/feminine counterpart, in numerology the number 10. The bible tells us that Mary and Joseph travelled the river Jordan, which is our spinal fluids; to be with Christ (Jordan means to 'Flow down or descend' – *also refer to quote from the Secret of the Golden flower regarding downward flow of seminal fluids*).

This is where the Christ seed is soaked and immersed in the spinal fluid (River Jordan) and baptized by John the Baptist undergoing a spiritual birth. The purpose of John's life was to prepare the way for Jesus; or in line with the Christ seed enlightenment; preparing the way for kundalini energy; to perfect the lower nature of man. John uses the symbolic aspect of water to prepare the matter of life.

To become the Christ there must be balance and order restored to your entire being. In other words you must be prepared for the kundalini awakening. Water baptism is about death of the old, the emergence of the new, in this case the death of your lower state to a rebirth to a Christ consciousness, the death of John the Baptist is symbolic of this. Water baptism is a symbolic burial, a death sentence to the lower self as we birth our Christ seed and higher consciousness.

There were many miracles attributed to Christ such as turning water into wine but that is again a bodily function. When water is taken and drank it merges and gets absorbed with and by our blood system to be used by our body and is thus turned into wine (Red wine is symbolic of blood as we see regularly in Holy-Communion celebrations the world over).

And so the story of the life of Jesus has begun, he is the breath of life, the oxygen of the body.

Or in astronomical terms 'prana' breathing a method of taking in sunlight at certain times such as sunrise and sunset, a human photosynthesis practiced by shamans and alike even today.

MORE ABOUT BALANCE OF OPPOSITES:

When we see pictures of both the head and feet of Jesus being rubbed by worshippers this is a message really telling us to balance our opposites so that they work together.

Another iconic image is Jesus on the cross with the letters INRI above his head. INRI means the four elements in Latin. The Latinised names of the 4 elements are:

Iam
Nour
Ruach
Iabesha

We are of course told different versions of this theme. The message here is one of telling us that such balance is the facilitator of equilibrium, the four elements, the four primal elements of human life on Earth needing to be balanced in order to reach the fifth element the ether, the father energy, the cosmos.

We all need to balance our own Samson and Delilah, light and dark. (Delilah derives from Dalketh meaning doorway of darkness).

In Hebrew the four elements are Yod-He-Wau-He (YHWH) = Yahweh. It is an intricate web of hidden knowledge and it gets more in-depth.

MORE BODILY SCIENCE:

It is said that Jesus held all things together and that he cured the sick. Again when we look into genetics we have a system called the Laminin which holds together our internal tissues and muscles and they are shaped like a cross (from where we get the word Laminate).

It is what the body uses to fight disease and it has an abbreviation of L.A.M.B.3 (3 being the 3 component parts of the atom), this is therefore the Lamb of God! *"And in him all things hold together"* – Colossians 1:17

IT'S ALL WITHIN US:

We are our own Salvation (Yeshua) and when we step out of spiritual darkness and into knowledge and the wisdom of the light we begin to realise this. This is the biblical story of Jonah and the whale, the whale was a symbol of spiritual darkness.

I will go more into the physical Jesus and what that means in the Egyptian teachings later on, as it goes even deeper than this in relation to our own salvation which is explained in the Pyramids and Sphinx of the Giza Plateau.

SODOM AND GOMORRAH:
The Location of the Place:

The body has an energy system called chakra's (wheel in Sanskrit) that is believed to be the spiritual power of the human body. At the base of our spine, Jacob's ladder, we have a serpent energy called the Kundalini; again in Sanskrit this means the coiled one. The Kundalini is the energy of fire that climbs Jacob's ladder activating each of our energy center's (Chakra's/Energy Seat) on its way to the top.

As it is activated and ascends upwards it destroys the lower chakras with its fire, the two lower chakra's are also known as Sodom and Gomorrah, based in the Kingdom of Earth, the lower body, as it approaches the Kingdom of Heaven, (Heaven meaning to heave up or to rise).

Heaven is referring to the upper body, where the higher level chakras are situated. The lower Earth chakras are the lower density chakras, the cause of low vibrational desires such as sexual appetite etc, this is the destruction spoken about in the Bible, the fabled land of Sodom and Gomorrah destroyed by fire due to the fornication and seedy lifestyle of its inhabitants, our own lower desires.

Sodom and Gomorrah is our own lowly places keeping us in the kingdom of Earth.

MOSES:
Drawn From The Water

Another famous character of the bible is Moses found in a basket in the river and was raised by adoptive parents. Moses means 'Drawn from the water' and 'Protection' in other languages. He led the Israelites (Israel-Elites- Elite means Gods chosen ones) across the desert and took on the Pharaohs face to face demonstrating miracles; the most well-known being the parting of the red sea that then closed on the Egyptian army as they followed in pursuit. He climbed the Mountain of Sinai and spoke with God who gave him 10 commandments, the law, which he was to give to the people who had gathered and made the long journey across dessert sands, the long and lonely wilderness. Moses was also involved in the plagues of Egypt for example the death of the firstborn children at the hands of the angel of death et al. But again did this really happen in the physical biblical sense?

If thousands of people had transited across the desert and had made such an exodus and had lived there for 40 years then there would be physical evidence of this. No archaeologist nor Egyptologist have ever found any artefacts or any physical remnants of such an odyssey.

And there is a valid and simple reason for that, it didn't happen.

Again the whole story of Moses is a metaphor for the inner workings of genetics within the human body. Before the Hebrew 10 Commandments (really the 10 emanations of self – Sephirot, the Hebrew Tree of Life) the Egyptians had a cosmic law of 42 Commandments (42 Ideals of Ma'at or 42 Negative confessions) from which we get the biblical 10, they are as follows: In the Egyptian book of the dead at death you pass 42 Judges:

There are also 42 names in the Gospel of St Matthew's version of the genealogy of Jesus and the number 42 is the number that Kabbalists believe God used to create the universe:

And it was the deliberately structured forty-two stages of the Israelites' from Sinai to the Plains of Moab - it was a journey marking their conflict with the dessert and had the will of God for Israel's future (Numbers 33:1-49):

In numerology 42 is a significant number:

Transgressions Against Mankind

1. I have not committed murder, neither have I bid any one to slay on my behalf;

2. I have not committed rape, neither have I forced any one to commit fornication;

3. I have not avenged myself, nor have I burned with rage;

4. I have not caused terror, nor have I worked affliction;

5. I have caused none to feel pain, nor have I worked grief;

6. I have done neither harm nor ill, nor I have caused misery;

7. I have done no hurt to man, nor have I wrought harm to beasts;

8. I have made none to weep;

9. I have had no knowledge of evil, neither have I acted wickedly, nor have I wronged the people;

10. I have not stolen; neither have I taken that which does not belong to me; nor that which belongs to another; nor have I taken from the orchards, nor snatched the milk from the mouth of the babe.

11. I have not defrauded, neither I have added to the weight of the balance, nor have I made light the weight in the scales;

12. I have not laid waste the ploughed land, nor trampled down the fields;

13. I have not driven the cattle from their pastures, nor have I deprived any of that which was rightfully theirs;

14. I have accused no man falsely, nor have I supported any false accusation;

15. I have spoken no lies, neither have I spoken falsely to the hurt of another;

16. I have never uttered fiery words, nor have I stirred up strife;

17. I have not acted guilefully, neither have I dealt deceitfully, nor spoken to deceive to the hurt another;

18. I have not spoken scornfully, nor have I set my lips in motion against any man;

19. I have not been an eavesdropper;

20. I have not stopped my ears against the words of Right and Truth;

21. I have not judged hastily, nor have I judged harshly;

22. I have committed no crime in the place of Right and Truth;

23. I have caused no wrong to be done to the servant by his master;

24. I have not been angry without cause;

25. I have not turned back water at its springtide, nor stemmed the flow of running water;

26. I have not broken the channel of a running water;

27. I have never fouled the water, nor have I polluted the land.

Sins

28. I have not cursed nor despised God, nor have I done that which God does abominate;

29. I have not vexed or angered God;

30. I have not robbed God, nor have I filched that which has been offered in the temples;

31. I have not added unto nor have I diminished the offerings which are due;

32. I have not purloined the cakes of the gods;

33. I have not carried away the offerings made unto the blessed dead;

34. I have not disregarded the season for the offerings which are appointed;

35. I have not turned away the cattle set apart for sacrifice;

36. I have not thwarted the processions of the god;

37. I have not slaughtered with evil intent the cattle of the god;

Personal Transgressions

38. I have not acted guilefully nor have I acted in insolence;

39. I have not been overly proud, nor have I behaved myself with arrogance;

40. I have never magnified my condition beyond what was fitting;

41. Each day have I laboured more than was required of me

42. My name has not come forth to the boat of the Prince

HERE ARE THE BIBLICAL HEBREW 10 COMMANDMENTS:

1. "I am the Lord your God, who brought you out of the land of Egypt, out of the house of bondage. You shall have no other gods before Me.

2. "You shall not make for yourself a carved image, or any likeness of anything that is in heaven above, or that is in the earth beneath, or that is in the water under the earth; you shall not bow down to them nor serve them. For I, the Lord your God, am a jealous God, visiting the iniquity of the fathers on the children to the third and fourth generations of those who hate Me, but showing mercy to thousands, to those who love Me and keep My Commandments.

3. "You shall not take the name of the Lord your God in vain, for the Lord will not hold him guiltless who takes His name in vain.

4. "Remember the Sabbath day, to keep it holy. Six days you shall labour and do all your work, but the seventh day is the Sabbath of the Lord your God. In it you shall do no work: you, nor your son, nor your daughter, nor your male servant, nor your female servant, nor your cattle, nor your stranger who is within your gates. For in six days the Lord made the heavens and the earth, the sea, and all that is in them, and rested the seventh day. Therefore the Lord blessed the Sabbath day and hallowed it.

5. "Honour your father and your mother, that your days may be long upon the land which the Lord your God is giving you.

6. "You shall not murder.

7. "You shall not commit adultery.

8. "You shall not steal.

9. "You shall not bear false witness against your neighbour.

10. "You shall not covet your neighbour's house; you shall not covet your neighbour's wife; nor his male servant; nor his female servant; nor his ox; nor his donkey; nor anything that is your neighbour's."

So having established the origin of the famous 10 commandments let's analyze the Moses story itself.

Within the human body there is a water soluble protection around the cells of the body, this is called the 'Fluid Mosaic Membrane' Mosaic means Moses, (drawn from the water). So straight away you can see that Moses was not a real person it is yet another story of human genetic origin.

Also within the body when a cell or aspect of DNA is dying it tells the other surrounding cells around it so that they can avoid any contamination. They give off a red dye (red blood on the doors of the houses of the first born to escape the angel of death) which is a message to them called Mito-genetic radiation or Mito Reds. Angel means messenger and this is the meaning of that particular scenario, that message of cellular or DNA death is the angel of death spoken about within this story. We have lots of protons in the body, they make up 1/3 of the atomic balance of our cells carried in our blood stream, or should we say Bourne, which means to be carried. Proton gives rise to proto, meaning first, therefore we have the First-Bourne (first born) again a genetic basis, the Genesis, the 'Gene of Isis'.

We have enzymes that open up the double helix strands of DNA and go inside them to help repair and fix the damaged or corrupted cells/DNA. Once inside; to prevent any other disease following behind the enzymes or even to escape the cleansing process; they close up the double helix strands behind the enzyme itself, in effect trapping them. This is what is described when the red sea closes in on the Egyptian army after they have entered the water to follow Moses and his people.

Now moving onto the rest of the story.

Moses scaled Mount Sinai until he reached the top awaiting any message or direction from God. What he saw was a burning bush which spoke to him giving him his 10 commandments which he was to take back to his people at the bottom of the mountain; Sinai incidentally means Mountain of the Moon. A mountain represents a dwelling of holy being; god or deity.

The burning bush is the pineal gland, our third eye, ignited by fire, the Kundalini energy; which we have previously mentioned. (Or in modern day computer logos, Mozilla Firefox, a fox being the symbol of spiritual awareness and Mozilla also means Moses) In Judaic circles Jacob fought the angel on mount Penial and was shown the face of God, the Pineal gland, which this was referring to; is known as the face of God. Regardless of religion they are referring largely to the same subject.

Moses first climbed the Mountain, the spine and reached the top of the mount (holy place); the skull within our head to reach the burning bush (pineal gland and enlightenment) obtaining the divinity of God. Mount Sinai also has several other names and is identified with mount Horeb which means to burn or to glow and also "Har Bashan," the latter word being interpreted as though it were "beshen" which means "with the teeth".

The signification of a tooth is the exterior intellectual and therefore natural truth. The teeth have this signification because they grind like a mill and therefore prepare the food which is to nourish the body; in this case the food which nourishes the soul.

The food which nourishes the soul is intelligence and wisdom; the intelligence and wisdom which is called spiritual and celestial food.

From this it is plain to see that the teeth signify the exterior understanding. What the exterior understanding is can be seen from what was shown just above concerning the interior understanding. That the teeth signify natural truth, which belongs to the exterior understanding.

When we are told of biblical quotes such as Jesus says, in Matthew 6:22 If your eye be single your body will fill with light, he is really saying that enlightenment to your mind will begin with the pineal gland, the burning bush.

God instructed Moses to throw down his staff and when he did it became a serpent, this is really talking about the spine and Kundalini energy.

From the visitation to Moses we now have the globally famous 10 commandments, ment meaning mind, therefore to command the mind, which he was to later smash in anger, where we get the expression breaking or to break the law. But just what is it actually referring to?

Again this, as you would expect from a word containing mind, is referring to the Brain. The stones are the two hemispheres of the human brain, the left and right side, the higher and lower mind (Taurus = Lower mind and Aries = higher mind, in medical astronomy). They are separated by cerebral fluids and blood, they are a red sea and to make the exodus from the lower to the higher mind; a natural stage of enlightenment; we must cross our own the red sea... does this sound familiar? The red sea is our blood stream and the biblical crossing is symbolic of our own journey of consciousness, the inner Passover to a new mind. It is the Corpus Collosum which is a term for the region of the human brain that connects the left and right cerebral hemispheres.

When kundalini is raised up the spinal column, the division between the lower man and your higher nature takes place, literally transforming our old way of thinking through a spiritual gateway, causing a parting of our energy waves.

Israeli Professor Zeev Herzog said ''after 70 years of intensive excavations, the evidence shows that there was no exodus from Egypt''.

Not a physical one at least but an internal one; yes. Moses allegedly spent 40 days and nights in the wilderness but again this is symbolic.

The number 40 represents transition or change; the concept of renewal; a new beginning. The number 40 has the power to lift a spiritual state; in this case the exodus and crossing between our hemispheres

When you understand this genetic language it becomes clear that there are countless of so called Jesus and other quotes that can only be referring to one thing, that being the internal workings of the human bodily system.

Moses took the laws of God and brought them down the mountain to show the people and to tell them that this is how they should live their lives, to honour Gods law. When he saw them they were carving Bulls as fake Gods and this is when he smashed the tablets in anger at them. But what is this really telling us?

It is saying that humanity is operating in the lower mind (Taurus) and is not yet ready for the higher mind (Aries) and that is still relevant today when we see the actions of many and their mindless thought patterns of destruction and contempt. Those of the higher mind don't need laws they have a finely tuned conscience.

NOAH
(And The ARK)

Another world famous character of the bible was Noah, the man tasked with building a gigantic ark for all the animals of the world to board in order to be saved from the impending flood. He was to gather all the animals in two's; both male and female; so that they could procreate post flood and flourish the Earth once again. I often have mental images and one of those is of penguins packing their suitcases in Antarctica and waddling all the way to the Middle East to board the ark, of course unable to fly there. When you see things in this way you can then see the absurdity of the Noah story, but again only in the literal physical sense but not when you again attach a bodily connection to it, then it becomes very plausible.

Noah means comfort and comfort and protection is what a baby; whist in its mother amniotic sack gets; protection from the outside world until the mother's waters flood, bringing the child out into a new world.

According to the Jewish Talmud it takes 40 days for an embryo to be formed in its mother's womb. And when we are told that it rained for 40 days this is talking about a mikveh (a bath used for the Jewish rite of purification) of which must be filled with 40 se'ahs; which is a measure of water. Immersion in a mikveh is the consummate Jewish symbol of spiritual renewal.

DNA is the building blocks of life and they are built upon base pairs, some genealogists actually call this miracle the 2 by 2 of chromosomes and this is what the story of the animals that went in two by two really means, it is the base pairs of human DNA.

Base pair - Dictionary Definition:

"A base pair is a unit consisting of two nucleobases bound to each other by hydrogen bonds. They form the building blocks of the DNA double helix, and contribute to the folded structure of both DNA and RNA. Dictated by specific hydrogen bonding patterns, Watson-Crick base pairs allow the DNA helix to maintain a regular helical structure that is subtly dependent on its nucleotide sequence. The complementary nature of this based-paired structure provides a backup copy of all genetic information encoded within double-stranded DNA. The regular structure and data redundancy provided by the DNA double helix make DNA well suited to the storage of genetic information, while base-pairing between DNA and incoming nucleotides provides the mechanism through which DNA polymerase replicates DNA, and RNA polymerase transcribes DNA into RNA. Many DNA-binding proteins can recognize specific base pairing patterns that identify particular regulatory regions of genes"

It was not a titanic sized ship that was able to carry every species of animal, mammal and insect on the planet. Again it is talking about something much more simplistic, yet magnificent; the human body. As the baby leaves the womb during child birth it enters a new world post flood, after the breaking of its mother's flood waters where a new life begins. A mother's heartbeat, (the heart being an electromagnetic generator), is amplified within the amniotic sac. It is an electrical circuit which becomes more apparent when we analysis the word ar(k) the K is the symbol of an electrical circuit/relay and Biphasic electrical currents stimulate promoting both proliferation and differentiation of fetal neural stem cells. We are an electromagnetic computer. In much the same way that the Ark of the Covenant is the brain and its electrical system, covenant is a contract and that contract is with the higher mind (ment), which is a transmitter and receiver to a higher plane.

The story is about the body and not a man with a gigantic ship.

MARY MAGDALENE

Mary Magdalene has been associated with the gospels, travelling with Jesus, being the first to witness the resurrection of Christ et al. She has been spoken of as a whore by certain male dominated Churches and even the wife of Christ by others. She has been the focal point of famous films such as Angels and

Demons by Dan Brown as carrier of the San-grail, the bloodline of Christ. But again was she a real person?

Keeping in line with the course of this book you'll not be too surprised when I say no she wasn't. Instead she is also a part of human consciousness sitting in the brain under the title of 'Amygdala'. Mary Magdalene was referred to as an illuminatrix or illuminator drinking the love (light) causing it to ray outwards in abundance. The Amygdala; being close to the Thalamus (Jesus) in the brain witnessed the crucifixion and resurrection from the tomb (cerebellum) and therefore understood the origin of our real spiritual light which she used to enlighten others. The Amygdala produces advanced positive emotions; fear response; lust and memories of sexual experiences and with the use of neuron stimulating chemicals can open us up to higher level experiences.

Both the Amygdala and Pineal glands of the human brain are a gateway to higher dimensions. Sitting there as part our limbic system the Amygdala witnesses everything; as did the fabled Mary Magdalene. Another biblical character was Mary of Bethany who approached Mary Magdalene telling her of Jesus's desire to see her.

This is the smaller Amygdala of the brain, Beth means house and the mind is known as the house, in other words Mary of the house/mind.

Mary Magdalene, Mary of Bethany and Mother Mary are known as the three Mary's. Mary Magdalene was not a real person but a part of each and every one of us and our consciousness system.

MARY & JOSEPH

As I have already alluded Mary and Joseph are the Ida and Pingala; the two opposite energy transistors each side of the human body playing an activate part in the role and life of the Christ seed. The image of Mary and Joseph seated at opposite ends of the manger can be interpreted as Ida and Pingala nadis, or energy channels for the flow of feminine and masculine energies. When the two energies become balanced, they wake up Kundalini, the divine energy. Kundalini begins its accent up through Shushumna nadi, which is between Ida and Pingala.

As Kundalini ascends it provokes the birth of the divine consciousness, the divine child, the Christ; Seth/Seph also means 'seed' and Jo means 'God shall add' or 'he will add'. Our Christ seed; the spiritual son; is born in Bethlehem when we are 12, which is the age that according to the bible Jesus started his father's work.

In the Solar plexus (Bethlehem) there is a thimble shaped depression; a cave or manger also known as the fish, which is the symbol of Jesus who was also called the 'Fisher of men'! This is where the seed/holy child is deposited; born of Immaculate Conception or 'Virgin birth'. The Ida and Pingala are nerves that go down the spinal column with the Pingala coming from the Pineal gland and the Ida from the pituitary gland; they are seated at opposite ends of the manger around the Christ seed in a manger in Bethlehem.

The Ida and Pingala converge through the 'Semi-Lunar-Ganglion the cranial nerves. The biblical walls of Jerico are the skull surrounding the brain and nerves, the bone walls of reinforcement protecting the region. Jerico was sieged by the 12 tribes of Israel in biblical legend but this is really the 12 cranial nerves.

Jerico means Moon/City of the Moon. The Ida has lunar connections and Mary means water which is controlled by the Moon. The Moon, in astronomy, is the guardian of the first heaven when a soul seeks to ascend. It rejects many of them and returns them from whence they came, from where we get the expression 'monsters' (Moon-star). All in all once again these characters are talking about the inner workings of the body and mind.

There are other characters that I could have highlighted, especially those of biblical fame, pointing out that the whole concept of these hidden systems are really about self and the body and its functions as we strive for a better height. But I think that the point has now been made and we can move on. What the bible is talking about with these characters is what is happening within the Human body. We are all the Christ, we are all Mary and Joseph, we are all Moses and Noah and we are all protected by the walls of Jerico.

6

THE LORD'S PRAYER (PRAAYER) - THE REAL MEANING

The Lord's Prayer (Praa/Pharaoh = Great House/The Human Mind & Yer = place/location/the ground/Earth) is iconic within Christianity documenting a time and conversation when Jesus spoke to his father and its words are recited religiously by the sheep, the followers of Christ.

(Jesus and his crown of thorns; representing the end of terrestrial serpent awakening, prior to entering the cosmos)

But again are we missing something that has been put out there to be missed or even more importantly to be deciphered and found in order for us to achieve a greater understanding of self?

When we analyze the words and take a deeper look at their meanings and what they are in fact telling us we can again see a genetic-human consciousness message that all we ever need is within ourselves!

LORD'S PRAYER – Traditional Version:

"Our Father, who art in heaven,
hallowed be thy name;
thy kingdom come;
thy will be done;
on Earth as it is in heaven.
Give us this day our daily bread.
And forgive us our trespasses,
as we forgive those
who trespass against us.
And lead us not into temptation;
but deliver us from evil.
For thine is the kingdom,
the power and the glory,
for ever and ever.
Amen"

This is my interpretation of its meaning based on the theme of this book and my research into hidden meanings and symbols of religion generally.

Our Father – *The Father Energy, the Ether – the original creator*
Who art in Heaven - *(higher places of the body) - art = a skill at doing a specified thing, typically one acquired through practice, namely consciousness and the internal wisdom.*
Hallowed *(Halo/Light)* be Thy Name *(Identity-Nature-Divine Frequency).*
Thy Kingdom Come *(Higher Mind through art of practice),*
Thy Will Be Done,
On Earth as it is in Heaven – *(opposing opposites become one through kundalini energy travelling from Earth, lower chakras to Heaven- Higher chakras and the balancing of both lower and upper chakras our own Heaven and Earth within).*
Give us this day, our daily bread - *(Christ Seed born in the solar plexus (Bethlehem meaning House of bread/Lord means Bread-giver).*
And forgive us our trespasses
As we forgive those who tresspass against us - *(those who enter our house-mind/temple without authority – this also has relevance to the Garden of Eden and the forbidden fruit/knowledge stored in the temple/head),*

And lead us not into temptation - *(don't let us be lead away from our purpose)*
But deliver us from evil - *(Apophis, the serpent of darkness in Egypt who fought with the Sun/light each night – also symbolic of George and the Dragon),*
For thine is the Kingdom, the power and the glory, forever and ever Amen.
Amen = Amun, meaning Hidden, this is talking about the hidden power of the mind, mind over matter – on Earth as it is in Heaven (simply mind and matter, the physical and mental aspects of self-combined and merged together as one ultimate power)...

The verses are telling us that our cosmic and divine connection is within Golgotha, the place of skulls, our own Mind…the Ark of the Covenant.

Many religions know the importance of this human feature, the third eye system, and we can see this in such names as the 'Vatican' which derives from Vatika meaning third eye. At the Vatican you can see many pine-cone structures dotted around, the pine-cone is the Pineal gland. All religions; unbeknown to the followers; and the famous influential cultures; worship the planets especially the Sun, as did the Egyptians, but not only the visible solar sun but another sun, a much deeper one, which I will detail soon. The word Catholic for example means 'Universal' which has planetary and much larger connotations.

(Endocrine system secretly hidden within this religious symbol)

7

ZECHARIA SITCHEN – THE SCROLLS; THE TRUTH...

There are many ancient cultures of great knowledge and understanding, such as Babylon and Sumeria, which is the modern day Iraq and others. For those who are familiar with author Zecharia Sitchin you will be aware that he translated and gave the world many books following his interpretation of the Sumerian scrolls.

(The late Zecharia Sitchin holding Sumerian scrolls)

They too, like the Egyptians, spoke in a clandestine way about consciousness, only the characters changed and this will become more evident when we reach the Egyptian section in more detail later.

But in the same vein that religious books like the bible are a mistruth this is my belief of Sitchin's translation which is giving a physical story but yet actually referring to a deeper esoteric reality. Before we move onto Egypt let's analyze Sitchin's work with just a few highlights of what he said. Sitchin mentioned extensively planet X, often called Nibiru. It is no coincidence in my mind that the Egyptian name of the planet Venus is Neb-Heru and the frequency of the orbit of Venus activates the Pineal Gland, sounding like an inner –bell; one of the reasons Venus was so important to the ancients, observed as it transited across the night skies.

Many people the world over are seeing a planet like object next to the Sun and claim that this is planet X. There are two natural explanations for this, they are natural phenomena. Firstly Sundogs, their official name Perihelion, which occurs when the sun is on the horizon; the sun's light shining off ice particles in the atmosphere. Secondly we have a natural phenomenon called Hunters Moon which occurs when the Moon is setting and the Sun is rising, and because the Moon is a reflection of Sunlight it looks like two Suns in the sky at the same time. Sitchin also goes into the Anunnaki and Anu. The first scenario however seems most likely as Hunters Moon only appears at certain times; which has not always coincided with witness testimonies of seeing the event on certain dates.

Anu is referring to the ultimate physical universal atom of creation, it is the center of the two joining rings of the figure 8 (infinity). He also details two characters called Enki and Enlil, the snake brothers.

This is the double helix of human DNA shaped like two snakes coiled together. The Enki and Enlil story and the battles between them; are the two opposing opposites, EG left and right, good and bad, basically the mastering of duality. Anunnaki means to change the atom for the better, maybe this is referring to genetic tinkering, a genetic upgrade of some kind, but that is for another time.

But when speaking of Enki and Enlil, the Gods of Earth & Sky we are talking about on Earth as it is in Heaven, the two aspects of self, lower and upper chakras and so on.

The picture at the start of the chapter, which is now famous amongst Sitchen followers has a hidden meaning, again like the Egyptian pictures that contain the same message, this will become more evident later when I go more into specific details. But this picture is representing consciousness and this is how.

(The Sumerian God Enlil)

The wings of the God are the 'Lateral Wings' of the Cerebellum, in fact they depict the two hemispheres of such (Cerebellum means Little Brain). The Two hemispheres are separated by the Vermis which is Latin for Serpent, indicated in the picture by the serpent God Enlil.

As you can see from the picture the God is carrying a Pine-Cone which is the Pineal Gland (Pine-cone gives us the word Pineal) therefore the whole picture is telling us about our Endocrine system (Endocrine = secreting within) our third eye consciousness. Many do not know this; many think this is what Sitchen describes as the Anunnaki Gods, as per his deciphering of the Sumerian scrolls. The mining for Gold that he spoke of would be referring to searching for enlightenment. The Pineal Gland's importance is shown through mythology too with the likes of one-eyed Cyclops and in Norse Mythology with the God Odin who traded an eye at the well in exchange for wisdom; this is symbolic of the pineal gland also. It is celebrity culture to cover one eye on magazine pictures and alike, this is again eye of Horus, third eye symbology. The now famous Fleur De Lys; used by the likes of the Prince of Wales; is also the 3 component parts of the endocrine system. Did Sitchen know this and did he choose to simply not say, or was he oblivious to its message? Only he would have known his true intentions. Another striking thing about the translation is that Sitchen states that when the Anunnaki came to Earth they found life already here. It also states that it was the Sheti, the snake brothers, Enki and Enlil; who brought the Moon to where it is now from another part of the universe. Scientifically this is incorrect and cannot be true for these reasons. The Earth and Moon have the same Isotopes; chemical elements and were therefore made at the same time with the same materials. The Moon is exactly 400 times closer to Earth than the Sun and is exactly 400 times smaller than the Sun which gives us the illusion of an eclipse.

The Moon is a planetary stabilizer for Earth keeping her at a 23.5 tilt which enables Earth's oceans to be a liquid and gives us the 4 seasons. Without the Moon there is no life on Earth. The human body is influenced and has connections to the Moon especially the female body which is locked into Moon cycles.

Therefore the statement that life was already present when these Gods arrived cannot be true if they were supposed to have brought the Moon with them.

All the advanced ancient cultures knew one thing, human consciousness and awareness and how to achieve it, but none more so than the ancient Egyptians as you will very soon find out.

STONEHENGE:

And this esoteric information is widespread throughout the ancient cultures. Another famous and mysterious monument is Stonehenge in Rural Wiltshire in England. Again many have guessed at its purpose, I have found that its purpose was as follows.

The whole area of this region in England, which also contains Stonehenge itself, was believed to have spanned over several miles. Originally 700 stones may have been present in various locations within that region which looks different today from what it did then and it formed the shape of a serpent which can be seen from old sketches and references.

The number 700 is very apt as it represents the evolution of the microcosm, the seven principles of the man. It is the symbol of the Resurrection as an image of the Phoenix, this mythological bird that once burnt and reappeared out of its own ashes.

In Greek, the numerical value of Phoenix, FOINIX, gives us the number 700 = 500+70+10+50+10+60.

The Numerical value of words and letters is known as gemetria. The well-known adage the 'Phoenix from the flames' is really referring to Kundalini activation as it travels to the third eye and sets it alight with its energy of fire. According to the ancient Chinese a vital energy circulates through the body on the specific paths called meridians. This vital energy makes surface on the skin with more than 700 different points. It is essential in the balancing of this vital energy of the body.

Tall stones have seven bands of energy or ranges of energy. While the Earth Kundalini travels from the middle of the Earth up through the perineum and straight through the middle of the body and out the top of the head the Body Kundalini begins at the base of the spine and travels up the spine and out the top of the head. This requires preparation and balance and purity of the body in order to facilitate such a transition otherwise the process will be blocked and will fail.

These seven bands equate to and are connected to our chakras (Energetic chakra bands) and our ancient ancestors utilized a powerful circular Earth energy pattern known as a Primary Halo. It is a bodily tuning fork of balance and synergy.

It is highly magnetic and invariably consists of three concentric circles of energy and standing stones and mounds were sited upon them.

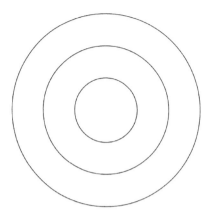

(Concentric Circle)

This is the reason why the ancients chose a circular design for their stone circles and mounds and sacred sites mark their location within the esoteric landscape.

Concentric means of or denoting circles, arcs, or other shapes which share the same centre, the larger often completely surrounding the smaller.

Blue stones were originally formed into an oval shape (the shape of our pituitary gland). But later the Bluestones were arranged in a circle between the two rings of sarsens and in an oval at the centre of the inner ring. Constructing Europe's unusual megalithic and Cyclopean architecture was based on a mysterious "technique" which involved tapping the strength of the "god within" by awakening the "Cyclopean" or Third Eye.

Preseli Bluestone (originally outer circle) activates the Soma Chakra, located at the hairline above the third eye. This is a higher resonance of the third eye, when activated the soma chakra opens metaphysical awareness and visionary ability. It also has to do with perception of the cycles of time and awareness and the workings of synchronicity.

When this chakra is functioning well it gives you the mental clarity necessary to achieve en-lighten-ment and promotes lucid dreaming. It unites the pituitary gland that governs physical function with the pineal gland, a transcendent spiritual awareness. Preseli Bluestone helps you connect to Earth energies and the wisdom of the Celtic Druidic peoples.

Bluestone assists you to move beyond time to access the past or future and this is the reason it was chosen.

A megalith should be regarded as a semiconductor 'macrochip' (large electronics opposite of microchip) which has the capacity to store and transmit energy. They are energy beams that connect all stone circles across the landscape; using Earth energy. Sited upon Earth energy geometries they absorb and transmit energy (Energy grids networks).

They are Geodetic-megalithic energy of which there are several in any stone circle.

They generate geodetic energies. The rising of Earth's Kundalini (Serpent of Light) that happens within and through us connects with the 'Unity Consciousness Grid.

To support our greatest well-being, and to make possible our evolution and spiritual awakening, we must allow ourselves (and our brainwave patterns) to breath in concert with mother Earth and with her natural cycle's moment-to-moment.

The Earth is a spherical receiver of cosmic energy (evolutionary intelligence) which directs our biological process and spiritual evolutionary unfoldment. The Earth re-radiates the cosmic information it receives from its core outward in complex longwave signals. We receive these signals via our spinal columns and cranial structures (a vertical antenna system).

The cranial cavity, the capstone to this antenna, captures this information and refocuses it to the pineal gland, a neuro-endocrine transducer in the centre of the brain, where it is then transmitted (via the hypothalamus) as signals that direct the pituitary gland, the master control centre of the Brain. These signals are further distributed via the rest of the neurological system.

In planetary harmonics the frequency of Venus activates the pineal gland and sounds like an inner bell. If we could suddenly see four-dimensionally, we would no longer find ourselves in the Earth plane, we would find ourselves in a different dimension -- the Venus plane – a dimension of the afterlife realms called by the same name as the three-dimensional planet Venus. All afterlife realms exist as afterlife dimensions inhabiting the same space just at different frequencies or vibrations. Tracking Venus also gave rise to the megalithic Yard (MY); a distance of 2.72 metres also known as 'Eulers number' which is a fraction short of PI.

Venus was important to the builders of Stonehenge and also in modern day society as it represents the Pentagram, taking a pentagram shaped orbit and is therefore connected to the number 5; the fifth element, the ether.

This is the real reason for Stonehenge, it was a cosmic power station to awaken the Consciousness of the individuals who were present, taking them to greater places using the energy and power of Earth transmitted through themselves as an antennae.

So there you have it, Stonehenge was an energy grid used to harness Earth's serpent Kundalini energy and in turn to transmute their own chakra system into cosmic consciousness, the God-Head or God-state. This is an ancient principle of enlightenment used by all the famous cultures that I have previously mentioned in this book. A linear channel of cosmic energy from the core of Earth through the finely tuned 'Human body' and into the ether during our Kundalini awakening.

This has been practised extensively throughout our ancient ancestral history and is still today by the initiates of certain organisations who have retained this in-depth knowledge themselves purely for themselves.
The general populous will never know this knowledge as they are falsely taught about their reality which is created for them by the same groups of initiates and 'Brotherhoods'.

The simple fact is we do not know about our self, we do not even consider our capabilities and we are never accurately taught about these things.

Until we understand ourselves we can never reach our true potential and we can never access our rightful inheritance namely knowledge.

We must understand that we are multi-faceted and multi-dimensional and we are the make- up of the stars, planets and the cosmos.

We have access to the codes that will transcend us to the 'Great Beyond' and back again should we wish.

And shortly I will take you to Egypt and will reveal to you their version of this knowledge!

8

THE NEW AGE – IS NOT THE ROAD TO ENLIGHTENMENT...

When I had my awakening in 2009 and realised that life and reality were much different to what I'd originally thought, I found myself amongst those of the 'New Age' genre, spiritual people and spiritual groups who had a more encompassing grasp of life than I found amongst those of the major religions which I never felt tempted by or attracted to despite its magnetic attempts. They accepted life beyond the physical plane and they acknowledged other forms of life both physical and metaphysical which fitted in very well with the experiences that I was personally having at the time; by the dozen; it has to be said.

So it made sense that I should enter this arena seeking answers to my questions and when I say it was a wonderful time of my life and indeed that of my wife's life, I genuinely mean it. It was a lighter side to the usual stresses and pressures of modern day existence and my energy, as it was put, was at many events in various capacities with ever growing frequency. I do accept that sometimes things happen for a reason and I do accept that we sometimes find ourselves in certain places and amongst certain people to pin-ball us to where we really need to be and this time for me was such an example; it enabled me to reach my real destination; albeit through many side roads.

However, I soon discovered that those who spoke the rhetoric through the New Age over-used saying 'Love & Light' were anything but from that place. They had little understanding of the balancing of oneself, the only way to reach true enlightenment. I had given talks at spiritual venues only to be asked why I had brought the dark into such a building because my talk went into detail about a global agenda that is heading towards us with ever growing pace. The opinion that you mustn't concentrate on the dark otherwise you'll attract it and yet without a thought never contemplated that if God created light then that creation must have been from a place of darkness, light being a designated place for visible particles to be seen. And never a thought was given to the fact that dark is really light that we cannot see, nevertheless it is still light, it is black light, the ether, undetectable to the human eye but it is all around us and it is the enabler of the manifestation we call visible light.

They however held a belief in Christ (cosmically known in New Age circles as Sananda) which in Sanskrit means aspect of Lakshmi, who is the feminine aspect of the Sun and there is no coincidence regarding the solar connection there. The prosperity card that the 'Angel Cards' featuring Lakshmi; used by the New Age; is really talking about the wealth of knowledge that is activated by the Sun (Angel Cards are messages from your angels; similar to tarot cards; but in a much lighter sense).

(The New Age, uniting all religions under one umbrella)

If there is one thing more irritating to me than the religious fabrications born from ignorance, that is the New Age quote of 'Love & Light'; not because I am against these things but because yet again it is a quote stated out of ignorance, blindly proclaimed from the voice of a mind-set of people who think they are enlightened. It makes me cringe at my deepest levels, more than any other statement out there.

Merely because it is simply repeated without research or understanding from a smiling face who heard it moments earlier and now wants to say it themselves; it sounds good.

The origins of these things are rarely looked into before the rhetoric is simply repeated time and time again by groups sitting in circles (Really Wicca Protective Circles) chanting and sending remote healing to various locations around the globe from a rented room in a town and city near you. A magic circle used by the Magi (magicians) the world over to create a sacred place to control reality and our understanding of it and from a Jehovah's Witness prospective a 'Watchtower'; yet this is another piece of information lost on them.

The New Age can be traced back to the 19th century with the Theosophy movement of Helena Blavatsky which resulted in the organisation 'Order of the Golden Dawn' (Sun) incorporating the Scottish Rite of Freemasonry and the practice of secret/occult magic!

At its 18th degree, the Scottish Rite of Freemasonry, has a motto of 'Love; Light; Life' The German Mother Temple of the Order of the Golden Dawn' also has the same motto. The New Age is a spin-off of Freemasonry and Magic (The magic of Light).

So as we feel the vibrations of realism, where illusions of grandeur are fading away from those who are actually developing themselves, let's leave behind the nonsense that provides just another branch of a tree called 'You've been misguided again' and let us actually learn just what it is we are really doing and saying.

You can never be an enlightened being without balancing your two aspects, the frequency we call dark & light, one of which is visible to us and the other, black light, that isn't. So don't be out of natural balance by denying 50% of your true essence by just focusing on one aspect, the light, which is in itself also very misunderstood.

The world is awash with mistruth and misunderstanding and it is a passion of mine to help people to realise that reality is often fake and that reality is created for us by our environment and our experiences by groups of people at the helm and apex of society that intend to deceive us and intend to keep us away from the truth. The least that we can do under the circumstances is make it a little more difficult for them by simply not just following but asking and finding and understanding the answers to our many questions and not stopping until we get what we seek.

After I had released an article containing this information I was contacted by an initiate of the 'Order of the Golden Dawn' who said this: (name protected)…

"Michael Feeley… Well Spoken… well researched… accurate and true. The news stories that say "It just wasn't in him." are so wrong…the truth is it is in all of us… people suppress and deny their yang side until it just burst uncontrollably. I was initiated into Golden dawn and Pranic Healing, who both used the slogan. In Buddhism and other disciplines…including Egyptian….The "Demons" you encounter on the trip to the afterlife are the dark energies that reside inside of you and you have not yet come face to face with…or dealt with".

Always question everything and always understand just what it is you are saying and ultimately doing. Enlightenment does not come from the denial of self. The New Age is not the road to enlightenment.

9
THE SECRETS OF THE PYRAMIDS: THE ANATOMY OF THE BRAIN

THE MYSTERY NOW REVEALED...

What would it have been like in ancient Egyptian society? The Pharaoh watching the Sun-Rise on the horizon (Horizon = Horus-Risen) each morning energizing the land of Egypt for another day with its Golden light.

Well I would guess that it was a system similar to what we have today, especially here in the UK, with interbreeding Royalty, marrying within their own family to keep their DNA pure; holding onto secret knowledge that only the worthy were entitled to know and using it for their own advantage. This usually being the establishment who run the day to day business, in modern day society; the knighted, the titled, the SIR, doing their bidding (Sir derives from Osiris and 'Arise' is the transit that the sun makes, it rises).

And of course the commoners like you and me who are the slaves suffer at the hands of the whip; or in the modern age; the slavery of debt and the imprisonment of body and mind due to a constant bombardment of low vibrational challenges.

But for those who had the knowledge, the walking Sun-Gods, the Pharaoh's and the Priests who went hand in hand; life must have been great. They believed themselves to be physical incarnations of the solar deities, such as Akhenaten, which means the living spirit of Aten, which is forever evidenced in their hieroglyphs and other symbolic and allegoric writings. Knowledge was a privilege and not a right; it had to be earned through worthiness and was not passed on lightly. Initiations were tough, many failed, only the strong succeeded. The temples were the location for greatness, the mind, the house of the God-like state (temple means 'Gods house)

They knew and understood the workings of our most inner-self and they practiced wholeness and divinity reaching the dizzy heights of enlightenment. They knew how to find and extract knowledge and wisdom from their own DNA/RNA that we can only do now by way of sophisticated and advanced technical scientific equipment, that we are told is a product of the 21ˢᵗ century.

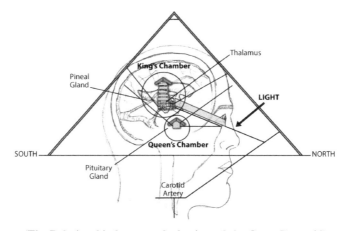

(The Relationship between the brain and the Great Pyramid)

And how did they do this? They must have had access to the same level of equipment that we do today. They also had knowledge of the 3 Wise men that form part of the human endocrine system (Secretion within) and they understood, unlike the New Age, that in order to reach wholeness and divinity the two lands, the opposing sides namely duality, which is the effect of a trinity, must be merged into one.

The merging of the two lands, the Sema-Tawy (Cemetery, so-called as it is the bridge between life and physical death) they tied the Knot as we do during marriage ceremonies today, the chemical marriage of King and Queen (which leads onto the King and Queen's Chamber of the Great Pyramid later).

There were 3 main pyramids at Giza, The great pyramid which is Khufu's pyramid (Khufu means 'Name of a Pharaoh' and in numerology this name has an expression/core number of 22, which is the number I continue to frequently see) Khafre's pyramid (Khafre is a variant of Khufu) and Menkaure's pyramid (Menkaure means 'Divine').

(The Pyramids Of Giza)

(Tying The Knot - The balance and marriage of opposites)

The 3 Wise-Men (also the 3 Kings/Stars of Orion's belt in astronomy); the Endocrine System, Yet another Holy-Trinity, stimulated by the 'Star of Bethlehem' Flower, a symbol of purity; known as the 'Bach' remedy. They are as follows:

PINEAL GLAND: The pineal gland, also known as the pineal body, conarium or epiphysis cerebri, (also relevant to the religious celebration called Epiphany (meaning Pineal Gland, which is an ancient Christian feast day and is significant in a number of ways; celebrating the baptism of Jesus by John the Baptist, which was in the River Jordan/Spinal Fluid)

The Pineal is a small endocrine gland in the vertebrate brain. The shape of the gland resembles a pine cone, hence its name. The pineal gland is located in the epithalamus, near the centre of the brain, between the two hemispheres, tucked in a groove where the two halves of the thalamus join. The pineal gland produces melatonin, a serotonin derived hormone which modulates sleep patterns in both circadian and seasonal cycles.

The Pineal Gland (face of God, from Hebrew story of Jacob fighting the Angel of Mount Penial) is also known as the 'Inner Light' which is indicated in Hindu by the Bindi placed as a 'Red Dot' between the physical eyes and in Egypt by the 'Black Dot' the Aten. And also the Hathor headdress, Hathor meaning House of Horus, the inner light; symbolised by the Egyptian sun between cow horns. Below is the Pineal Gland which gives rise to the Eye of Horus:

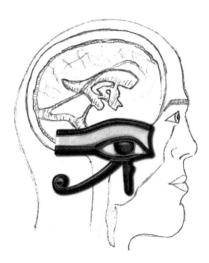

(The Pineal Gland within the brain and the Eye Of Horus)

The pineal gland also connects us to Earth's night and day cycles (Chronobiology cycles) secreting melatonin at night time which helps rejuvenate and rebirths us. If for example you work nights then you are in a permanent state of a death cycle as the body dies in the day and is reborn at night (cell production etc) I you are awake during normal sleep times then you cannot rejuvenate. It is stated by modern medical history that the existence of the Pineal gland has been known for circa 2000 years. The Egyptians knew about its existence many thousands of years prior to that! This gland secretes (from where we get the word secret) White & Brown fluids which was hidden within Judaism with the term for Israel, the 'Land of Milk and Honey'.

PITUITARY GLAND: (Oval shaped gland – see the likes of the Oval office at the White House, (Memphis, the original capital of Egypt means 'White Walls').

The pituitary gland, or hypophysis, is an endocrine gland about the size of a pea (where we get the expression Pea Brain) and weighing 0.5 grams (0.018 oz) in humans. It is a protrusion off the bottom of the hypothalamus at the base of the brain. The hypophysis rests upon the hypophysial fossa of the sphenoid bone in the center of the middle cranial fossa and is surrounded by a small bony cavity (sella turcica) covered by a dural fold (diaphragm) sellae). The anterior pituitary (or adenohypophysis) is a lobe of the gland that regulates several physiological processes (including stress, growth, reproduction, and lactation).

The intermediate lobe synthesizes and secretes melanocyte-stimulating hormone. The posterior pituitary (or neurohypophysis) is a lobe of the gland that is functionally connected to the hypothalamus by the median eminence via a small tube called the pituitary stalk (also called the infundibular stalk or the infundibulum).

Hormones secreted from the pituitary gland help control: growth, blood pressure, certain functions of the sex organs, thyroid glands and metabolism as well as some aspects of pregnancy, childbirth (Represented by Isis, Goddess of Motherhood), nursing, water/salt concentration at the kidneys, temperature regulation and pain relief. The Pituitary Gland also deals with fertility and lactation, hence another reason it is associated with Isis the Mother Goddess. The section between the Pineal and Pituitary Gland is called the 'Crystal Palace' for all you London football fans out there!

When we analyse the word Church we see that within it contains the letters UR and UR means Moon.

And why is the Church the Moon?

The moon shines with reflected light, it has no light in itself, it shines with the reflected light of the Sun. The Church reflects the light of Christ (Solar Sun) therefore the Church is representing the Moon.

We can also trace fertility cults back to the worship of the Egyptian Goddess Isis. Isis was associated with the Star Sirius 'A', but her cosmic appearance in the sky was the 'Moon'.In ancient Egypt, they had a Talisman/amulet called the 'Tyet' which was a similar shape to the famous 'Ankh'.

(The Pineal Gland within the brain and the Eye Of Horus)

Isis is symbolic of Motherhood and menstruation is the time when females are at child baring age and female body is closely locked into Moon cycles and also with the creation of the Lunar seed that I have mentioned previously.

We see many celebrities in modern pop culture and alike covering their right eye and exposing only their left eye. This is symbolic of the Moon (Isis) and her fertility cults. When the opposite occurs it is the symbol of Horus (Right eye only showing).

THALAMUS (PYRAMIDAS = Fire in the Middle - Tammuz in Babylonian Culture). The Thalamus is in the exact centre of the human brain and the great pyramid is in the exact centre of Earth's land mass and in addition to this the Sun is in the exact centre of the solar system, there seems to be a pattern emerging there.

The Thalamus (from Greek θάλαμος, "chamber") is the large mass of grey matter in the dorsal part of the diencephalon of the brain with several functions such as relaying of sensory and motor signals to the cerebral cortex, and the regulation of consciousness, sleep, and alertness. It is a midline symmetrical structure of two halves, within the vertebrate brain, situated between the cerebral cortex and the midbrain. The medial surface of the two halves constitute the upper lateral wall of the third ventricle. It is the main product of the embryonic diencephalon and it works with our Amygdala (Mary Magdalene).

CEREBELLUM: The cerebellum (Latin for "little brain") is a major feature of the hindbrain of all vertebrates. Although usually smaller than the cerebrum. In humans, the cerebellum plays an important role in motor control, and it may also be involved in some cognitive functions such as attention and language as well as in regulating fear and pleasure responses but its movement-related functions are the most solidly established. The human cerebellum does not initiate movement, but contributes to coordination, precision, and accurate timing: it receives input from sensory systems of the spinal cord and from other parts of the brain, and integrates these inputs to fine-tune motor activity. Cerebellar damage produces disorders in fine movement, equilibrium, posture, and motor learning in humans.

(The Death Mask of King Tutankhamun)

King Tutankhamun's (Tut-Ankh-Amun meaning strong and secret Genes, when we separate the words individually) Death Mask (which I saw at the Cairo Museum) illustrates several things given to us in plain sight. The rear of the headdress is the Cerebellum and our brain stem.

The front of the mask also shows the Cerebellum and its Lateral wings, separated by the Vermis, the serpent. It also shows the Vulture Goddess of Upper Egypt, Nekhbet and the Goddess of Lower Egypt, Wadjet, symbolic of the merging of the two lands, Upper and Lower Egypt by King Tutankhamun who was Pharaoh of both lands. The chin décor is the Uraeus or Greek Oura, meaning tail, in this case the tail of the serpent. The head of the serpent is masculine and the Tail is feminine, again we see the merging of opposites, masculine and feminine energy. We also have the serpent wisdom emanating from the third eye, the Pineal Gland; between the right and left eye, again opposites, male and female aspects of bodily control.

(The Scarab Beetle depicting wings of the Cerebellum)

The Scarab beetle also represents the Lateral wings of the Cerebellum and the hemispheres and the Aten, the Inner Sun/Light.

The 3 Wise-men are all overseen by the Cerebellum, the Bishop (meaning watcher/overseer) sitting on the Seat (Cathedral means seat/Energy seat/ chakras) and many Cathedrals once the human head is overlayed on their diagrams; show in a clandestine way the locations of these 3 endocrine glands, as does the greatest monuments of them all, the Great Pyramid.

Giza meaning border, representing Upper and Lower Egypt, North and South of the Nile Delta were merged by the Mind – Memphis, the symbolic Mind, with Heliopolis being the Heart and Thebes being the Tongue, HTM, Heart, Tongue and Mind. Memphis was the original capital city. And in line with frequencies; the Great Pyramids of Giza harness the very sound waves from the inner core of the earth which coincides with alpha rhythms produced by the human brain during meditation. The pyramids, Earth and the brain have the same range of frequencies. This is an advanced knowledge of sound/vibrational frequencies.

The Red & White flag of St George also represents upper and lower Egypt (Lower = Red, Upper = White) and good old English Pub names such as the Red Lion is symbolic of the Pharaoh's of Lower Egypt.

(Map of the River Nile)

All in all, we have a quadrant system that controls consciousness and within the Thalamus we have the 'Gate of God' the RU and as Jesus was reported to have proclaimed:

"No one comes to the Father except through me"… Th(RU) me! ('Me' in Sanskrit means 'Divine law').

This is where the Christ seed passes through the Thalamus and into cosmic consciousness, a Kundalini awakening as its energy explodes into the ether (father energy) having been c(RU)cified at the optic Chiasm, the crossing X (cross/chamber of Light) before returning to the father, the Neteru (NeteRU) the higher forces of nature that control the actions of mind and matter.

On Earth as it is in Heaven, the meaning of a 'New Testament' (Testament means Body and Mind). And Thought (Thoth) is the divine, the abstract concept that manifests into reality.

(The God Thoth, depicted with the head of a bird)

Thoth (Thought) is depicted in this picture with the head of a bird, birds were seen as the symbol of the element between Earth and Heaven and the souls/ spirits flight.

He is seen holding onto the Ankh, the key of Life which is really the process of 'DNA and Protein Synthesis. Protein synthesis is the biological generation of cells that bind with DNA.

When protein binds with DNA it loops and crosses around and over it and bonds in loop shapes before closing itself and tying itself off which is symbolised in the Ankh shape. The Ankh, key of life, is referring to DNA/Life DNA synthesis is the expansion and creation through the double helix DNA system of reproduction and revitalising of genetics, which again is essential within the term life.

The two serpents represent the Ida and Pingala (kundalini energy) travelling up the spine (Jacobs ladder) towards the Cerebellum hemispheres (wings) and the Aten (Pineal Gland, the Inner light) RA is the visible Sun (Sun-God) but the Amun RA is our hidden light, (hidden Sun) our inward journey to divinity and wisdom accessed through the invisible doors of our own Pyramid, to be activated into cosmic consciousness.

(The pyramid of the Third Eye, Pineal Gland)

And that leads nicely onto the Pyramids themselves in the desert of Giza. So what were these monuments all about? In acknowledgement that there are many other Pyramids around the world and indeed beyond, I will concentrate on Giza in Egypt.

GIZA PLATEAU:

The Giant Brain

So what have the scholars and Egyptologists of every decade and age missed?

When we watch TV documentaries about Egypt and the Pyramid and Sphinx of Giza (Giza meaning border) and are told that they were built for the burials of the Pharaoh's by Hebrew slaves who worked with primitive tools to carrying rocks and stones hundreds of tons in weight over rough terrain non-stop for 20 plus years, are we being deluded or deliberately deceived by the same groups and organisations that have tried to keep certain information a secret?

They know that the flux of enlightenment and the increase in the wisdom of humanity will come with the re-emergence of Egyptian knowledge.

This knowledge has stood the test of time and has been left written in the constructs of the Pyramids and Sphinx for us to decipher, it is a coded message of the grandest scale missed by the thousands of tourists who visit them each year only seeing, as I was told not to, the tourism of this great land and not her cosmic reconnecting message.

The Pyramids of Giza were not for burials at all; that occurred in Luxor (Luxor meaning Golden Light) in the Valley of the Kings.

Many, including Napoleon himself, have experienced strangeness when they ventured into certain places such as the Sarcophagus, they experience an almost out of body, astral travel like imagery, enabled by the remnants of such ancient rehearsals and practices.

They are experiencing the merging of two lands, the physical and metaphysical as aspects of themselves leave for a while; as to where, well that's anyone's guess.

The Pyramids and Sphinx are in essence a giant replica of the human brain and its endocrine system of enlightenment. This is the message that has been left for us to find: It is a massive statement (state of mind) left for us on the landscape telling us how to make that transition from man to the God-like mind, the RE.

The human brain has four regions/chambers namely the 'Ventricles' the four fluid filled chambers filled with Cerebral Spinal Fluid. The brain also has Four Regions: They are:

Cerebrum,

Diencephalon,

Cerebellum,

Brain stem

The brain also has 4 lobes one of which is the Occipital lobe which are lobes that are pyramid-shaped structures located at the back of the brain that receive and analyse visual information!

The great pyramid of Giza has four chambers, chamber meaning an enclosed space or room; namely

The Kings chamber,

The Queens chamber,

The Grand gallery

The Lower gallery

The Kings chamber and Queen's chamber are connected by the grand gallery, a bridge, or in the anatomy of the brain a 'Pons' meaning bridge, they are neural pathways or tracts that conduct signals from the brain down to the cerebellum and medulla, and tracts that carry the sensory signals up into the Thalamus and they connect the cerebellum to the pons and midbrain.

Again this is the inner most workings of our mind. There is a tower within the Kings chamber which is symbolic of the Djed, the spine of Osiris.

The top of the spine gives us the head and the consciousness arena.

In current spiritual circles we base our consciousness on the 7 chakras/chakra system:

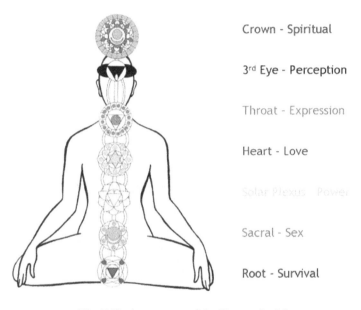

Crown - Spiritual

3rd Eye - Perception

Throat - Expression

Heart - Love

Solar Plexus - Power

Sacral - Sex

Root - Survival

(The 7 Chakra system of the Human body)

However the Egyptian based theirs on 9, with the addition of the Nasal chakra and the Carnell chakra and it is therefore no surprise that we have 9 Pyramids situated in the Giza Plateau.

The main 3 pyramids represent the Solar Cycle of RE, the Triple Triad, 3x3 = 9; there are 9 Pyramids at Giza. The number 3 means the perfection of the God-head and there are 9 levels of consciousness that operate together' hence why we have 9 pyramids in total leading us up to the 'Great Pyramid" the 'Great Mind' for the final enlightenment; our true eternal self.

The 9 levels of consciousness is a model of how the physical and none physical universe work together; which is including of the material realm and the 9ether forces of creation, a magical marriage.

(The Triple Triad)

The cross, amongst other meanings both genetic and astronomical, indicates the number 9 as such, which is the 9 chakra system:

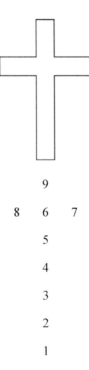

9

8   6   7

5

4

3

2

1

(6-7-8 are the three component parts of the third eye, the Essenbach code)

As already mentioned the number 9 represents 9ether, the forces of creation and higher existence, it is natures code the Fibonacci spiral that also generates Phi.

We have the opposing 6ether which is the chaotic forces based on our causation, the dualistic reality; both 6 and 9ther are represented by the Yin & Yang black and white spiral. The number 9 is also the enlightenment experience that is felt with the chakra awakening.

Everything in creation is a smaller version of the larger, the microcosm, macrocosm Russian doll effect and whereas the human body has an energy meridian system, so do countries and so do planets, meridian Leylines (Ley means law, and the line is the sacred shape of the partition).

When we look at the African Prime-Meridian chakra system we can see that Giza is its third eye:

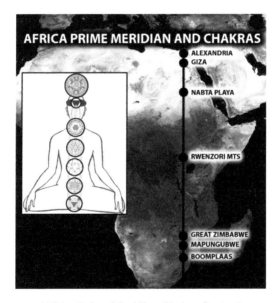

(Africa Prime Meridian Chakra System)

Alexandria which took over from Memphis as the eventual capital of Egypt is the Crown Chakra in this African meridian (Golden Pyramid Cap)

It has been proven that the Sphinx and Pyramids were once surrounded by water (Nile River – Nile means Yeor which is to shine).

The Pituitary Gland shines the same and that is no coincidence. Water erosion has been found beneath these monuments however water has not been in this region for 10,000 years, therefore the Sphinx at least and most likely the Pyramids must be at least this old.

Within the brain we have the water that surrounds and protects the brain called the Cerebrospinal fluid that comes into direct contact with our brains third ventricle and therefore the pineal Gland. It transports thoughts and information via Neuro-hormones and bio-chemical signalling to all parts of the body down this fluid system; which is what the picture of Thoth (Thought) is representing:

(Thought/Thoth travelling along the Cerebrospinal fluid)

The Monkey is symbolic of the Olfactory Tract in the brain that bares similarity to a Monkey.

The Olfactory Tract a nerve like, white band composed primarily of nerve fibres originating from the mitral cells and tufted cells of the olfactory bulb but also containing the scattered cells of the anterior olfactory nucleus. The tract, closely applied to the inferior surface of the frontal lobe, attaches itself to the base of the cerebral hemisphere at the olfactory trigone, beyond which it extends in the form of the olfactory striae that distribute their fibres to the olfactory tubercle and, in largest number, to the olfactory cortex on and around the uncus of the parahippocampal gyrus. It also deals with the sense of smell. The Olfactory Tract is a nervous system messenger.

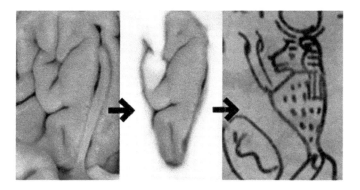

(Olfactory Tract of the Brain & Egyptian Picture)

The Pyramids were so placed as to replicate the waters of the Cerebrospinal fluids that also surround our endocrine third eye system.

(A depiction of the Sphinx submerged in water)

This was all inline with the mastering of opposites which leads to enlightenment and divinity the Pyramids and their structure is also very relevant to this fact.

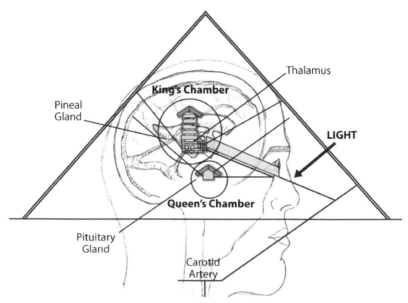

(Overlay of the King's Chamber in the Great Pyramid with the Human brain)

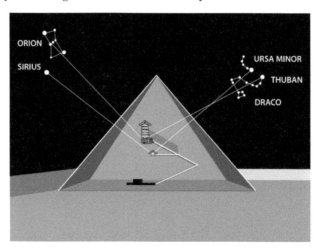

(The Great Pyramid shafts and their associated star constellations)

The merging of our opposites is the alchemical marriage of King and Queen which merge together as one in the Thalamus. Therefore the Pineal Gland (Osiris), the Pituitary Gland (Isis) and the Thalamus (Horus/Jesus) become one. It is no coincidence then that within the Great Pyramid we have the Kings chamber, Queen's chamber and the Thalamus (pyramid-fire in the middle) within this monument. The Great Pyramid is situated in the exact centre of Earth's land mass and the Thalamus is the centre of the brain.

The Pineal Gland (Kings chamber) within the Great Pyramid has a shaft that faces Orion (also Osiris) and the Pituitary Gland (Isis/known as the star chamber of Isis) faces Sirius A (also Isis) this is again the two opposites, male and female facing South.

Both the King's and Queen's Chamber were built rectangular which symbolises stability.

In the North (opposite of South facing shafts) we have two shafts facing Thuban in Ursa Minor and Draco, (The Pineal Gland is also known as the North Gate).

Draco is now called the Dragon, however in ancient Egyptian times it was called the Cobra/serpent and it was one constellation. In higher dimensional terms the serpent/dragon is symbolic of going beyond or leaving the solid world; sheading its skin; like the soul does as it leaves the physical skin; the body which can be done either living or otherwise.

The Egyptians did this in a physical living state most likely using knowledge given to them by a higher aspect of themselves which would have conversed with them in their out of body state.

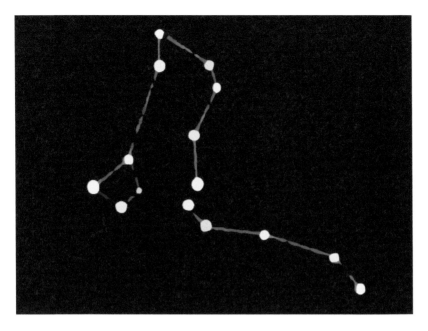

(Yin and Yang serpent, cosmic opposites)

The head of the serpent represents the male and the tail represents the female aspect of self, two opposite sides. This is also known as the 'Draconian Traverse', traverse meaning to lie across.

The Pyramid shape therefore is symbolic of two opposites mastered and merged as one as they reach the Pyramid capstone, where two become one and connect to divinity and enlightenment.

(The Tetrahedron)

The Pyramid, the alchemical symbol of fire, at its two bottom corners represent the two opposites merging into one at the Apex, the Gold Cap stone (Gold = symbolic of enlightenment); the Crown chakra. In Gemetria the number for light is 144 and there are 144,000 casing stones on the Great Pyramid, which is another enlightenment connection.

The soul having escaped the mummification process; its embodiment in the physical body, mummified by physicality now moves onto the afterlife, free as a bird, returning back to the ether, the supreme mind.

The pyramid base also represents the material/physical realm and the apex is a representation of the higher consciousness and the transit from one to the other.

The third eye will only open when 'conscious fusion' takes place between the opposites of our own consciousness. There would have been various initiations and rituals within the pyramids to induce this state; accessed most probably through the guardian of higher knowledge, the Sphinx.

The transition from unconscious matter to conscious existence with the mastery of this world and its duality; which is the symbolic meaning behind the legendary Phoenix from the flames.

Reaching the mental state (Ment-Al = mind of God). The mind relates to the brain, the greater mind, the mental, relates to the higher consciousness state, RE.

So; in keeping with theme of the balance of opposites there are many Egyptian statues that are clearly holding onto two cylinder shaped metal rods, one in each hand. The foot position of these statues is also of relevance. When we see the left foot more prominently forward it's of matriarchal significance and when we see the right foot more prominently forward it's of patriarchal significance.

But going back to the rods these are what are known as the 'Wands of Horus' and they were metal cylinders filled with various special materials and quartz crystals of differing sizes to enhance their psychic and mental ability as well as the balancing of their chakras, bringing harmony to their physical vessel and healing by regulating the energy balance of the body and they were a tool for attainment and unsurprisingly enlightenment.

The Wands of Horus take the form of two hollow cylinders made of copper and zinc for right and left hands respectively. This is important because the link between metal and hand is tightly bound up with the functions of the left and right hemispheres of the brain. Copper was held in the right hand and this symbolised the Sun (male energy) and the zinc was held in the left hand and this symbolised the Moon (female energy) and required the fundamental balance of the two.

 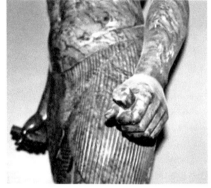

(The Wands of Horus - Copper held in right hand, Zinc held in the left)

All external and internal dimensions of the Wands of Horus conform strictly to the proportions of the Golden Section. This is of fundamental importance for the existence of resonant interaction between the cylinders and the user. To work effectively the Wands of Horus need to attune themselves to the organism, while the user's organism for its part should also attune itself to the Wands of Horus. Such interaction is only possible when the cylinders conform to the proportions of the Golden Section, also known as the Golden mean or golden ratio which is connected to the Fibonacci numbers and the golden section in nature, art, geometry, architecture, music and even for calculating pi.

The height of Wands of Horus is attuned to the pyramid and the diameter of the Wands is designed to be tuned to the Earth 'Eigenfrequency' which is a natural frequency; an inner frequency and a self-frequency.

When we delve into ancient advanced knowledge of universe and self we cannot but help stumbling across mathematics, sound and frequencies. This is because the very fabric of existence is universal mathematical code.

But there is a frequency significant to the ancient Egyptians and that is 432 Hertz.

432 Hertz is the Godlike state, a perfect frequency and when we use mathematics we get from this number the formula 4+3+2 = 9; 432 Hertz and Hertz means the amount of oscillations per second.

The number 9 is the enlightenment experience and this is the reason we have 9 Pyramids at Giza, it is a mathematical formula for the God frequency 432 hidden in secret code.

This frequency releases DMT from your pineal gland which makes it easy to go straight into the avatar state. An Avatar is a manifestation of a deity or released soul in bodily form on earth; an incarnate divine teacher.

DMT is a Psychedelic serum within the brain taking us into a spiritual mode. Chants at the right frequency help release Dimenthyltryptamine (DMT) which is a hallucinogenic drug that can be produced by the brain especially during REM sleep. The Egyptians used vowel sounding chants to invoke certain reactions to enhance this practice.

432HZ is a perfect balanced tone that helps you to grow Metaphysically. The diameter of the moon is precisely 2160 miles which is exactly 432 x 5. The diameter of the sun is 864.000 miles which is 432.000 x 2. The number 432 is also found in the patterns of planet orbits.

Pythagoras (570 - 495 BC) was a Greek philosopher, mathematician, astronomer and scientist.

He was credited for originating the "music of the spheres" theory which states there are musical intervals (mathematical ratios) found in the distances and sizes of the planets and how they moved around one another. It gave name to the Pythagorean Tuning scale which turns out to produce the A=432 Hz! 432 is encoded into the very workings of the cosmos.

Listening to the 432Hz frequency resonates inside our body, releases emotional blockages and expands our consciousness.

432Hz is the 'Miracle Tone' and raises positive vibrations and it is a healing frequency. 432 Hertz is pitching 'A' on the musical scale.

A = 432 Hz, known as Verdi's 'A'; is an alternative tuning that is mathematically consistent with the universe. Music based on 432Hz transmits beneficial healing energy, because it is a pure tone of maths fundamental connection to nature. Verdi was a composer and it is said that the famous composers tuned their music and symphonies to this tone and frequency also. The letter 'A' is also the Pyramid shape and would resonate with the same tone and frequency.

Archaic Egyptian instruments that have been unearthed are largely tuned to A=432Hz. 432Hz unites you with the universal harmony. This tone is closely related to the universe around us, it is the pitch of energy release, chakra tuning, relaxation and meditation and healing. 432 hertz is enlightened consciousness.

(The Egyptian instrument, the Sistra)

Ancient Egyptian instruments such as the Sistra or sistrum are tuned to this frequency and its importance can be seen in many carvings and hieroglyphs shown in the Temples of Egypt.

The number 216 is the number of the beast, man and is one octave below 432 hertz. In the bible the number of the beast is 666, but if we make this mathematical equation 6x6x6 we get 216. If we take the Hebrew letters and their numerical value to create geometry they fit into the 216 outline triangle, which again is the Pyramid shape.

If the octave of man is 216 then the octave higher is 432, the Egyptians were taking themselves from man to God, 216+216=432.

(The letter 'A' forms the pyramid shape)

Going back to Verdi's 'A' in the Hebrew language the word Aleph as in the first letter of the alphabet, means 'Father' or the head of royalty (king). Aleph has the gemetria of 1, in other words at 1 with God as the material realm, the four sides of the Pyramid, turn into a connection with the ether, the fifth element at the capstone, where we go from man to God-like The significance of the 'Head of Royalty' is contained in the Earlier passage regarding the word Pharaoh meaning 'Great House' which in other words is 'Great Mind'.

342 is a sacred universal number that other cultures have harnessed too. For example at the Buddhist Borobudur Temple in Indonesia there are 432 Statues of Buddha which is an esoteric reference to this number. Even Tibetan singing bowls are set at this frequency. The Lotus flower is significant in these culture as well as in Egypt where in addition to enlightenment the Egyptians also saw it as the joining of Lower and Upper Egypt due to its intertwining stems.

It brings me right back to the quote from Pythagoras that "All is number"

And to put an extra synchronicity or three to this when I was writing this passage I just happened to look down, for no reason, at the word count and it was 432 at that stage! And shortly after I got a social media request to like someone's page which was called, you guessed it, 432 Hertz!!! (I took photos of both).

Then later that evening, a few hours after, I was walking down a set of stairs whereby I heard a sound I can only describe as a whoosh inside my head and in a split-second I saw a Pharaoh of Egypt in full Golden Serpent headdress.

It happened very quickly and ended very soon after it started, maybe a second or two at the most. I cannot say If I had morphed into him or if he was walking alongside me, but I could see him from my walking angle, as if it was me and also from a sideways angle, therefore it was a multi-dimensional view, seeing the same object from multiple angles at the same time!

He was shorter than me and had dark skin, looking straight ahead and walking in silence with a stern face, but with purpose and importance.

(The appearance was strikingly similar to this picture)

We have been left a wonderful advanced knowledge by our ancient ancestors and as the full picture reveals itself piece by piece I sit here in wonderment.

The Pyramids represent consciousness and how to reach it. Not only was one of the pyramid shafts facing Orion/Osiris to show us the connection to the Pineal gland (also relevant to the Kings chamber) but also the three main pyramids of Giza are aligned to the constellation of Orion too, to reinforce this message.

THE SPHINX

In Greek Sphinx means Sphingo to restrict as in their version of the Riddle of the Sphinx with those who fail being strangled.

However in Egyptian Sphinx means 'to combine', and this is relevant in several ways as such. As part of enlightenment the Egyptians were combining opposites into one. There is of course also an astronomical version with this representing the merging of the Zodiac with Leo and Virgo, giving indication of the times of the Procession of the Equinox; but that's for another time.

The Sphinx is also a representation, in its original form, of the tetramorph, (Tetra = four and Morph = shape) which are the four elements (or biblical 4 apostles) Fire, water, Air and Earth.

The Sphinx may have originally looked different to what it does to today with sabotage and decay, but it is a symbolic arrangement of four differing elements, or the combination of four disparate elements in one unit.(in New Age circles this is also representing the Archangels Michael, Uriel, Gabriel and Raphael)

They are elements as simple substances which provide the primary components of the human body. The four elements are sometimes referred to as "primary matter;" and matter is the physical world that the Egyptian initiates mastered at the point of cosmic consciousness.

The movement of these four elements is continually taking place, so that change is a continuous process within the human body. The "Living Creatures" or the 4 beasts, as the tetramorph is known, were placed at the entrance to the "Garden of Eden" (body) and were the protector of the 'Throne of God'. (Heaven – Ether, or in physical terms the higher chakras/seals/energy seats).

As already discussed in a previous chapter the Garden of Eden is the Human body and the sphinx/4 beasts is the protector of the higher wisdom and knowledge (pineal/penial = Face of God).

In Egypt upon the mummification process we have the Canopic Jars (Canopic derives from Canopus – a land in Lower Egypt) with body parts placed within and protected by the 4 Sons of Horus: The 4 cardinal points of the compass. The 4 sons of Horus are as follows;

Imsety

Qebehsenuf

Hapy

Duamatef

Also as previously discussed the Pyramid, directly behind the Sphinx (and therefore shielded/protected by), is the endocrine system that connects us to

God, the sphinx is the protector of the Throne of God, the God-mind, our God-like consciousness. Throne of God is also another expression for the Pineal gland. The Atef crown worn by many Egyptian Gods is symbolic of the brain opened out and exposing the component parts of the third eye endocrine system. Atef means 'His might'.

God; we are told in the biblical scriptures; is light and our pineal Gland is our inner light, the Amun Ra, the seat of the soul. Its divinity must be protected and this is the message given to us by this symbolic guardian in the desert. The human mind, replicated by the Great Pyramid, in the internal sense is the natural and rational mind where intelligence and wisdom reside, the human mind, the 'Throne of God'…The initiates were protecting the wisdom and the key to divinity for the worthy.

(The Sphinx at Giza in Egypt)

The Egyptians, through and with their magnificent monuments, were showing us the anatomy of the human brain, a gigantic replica of our Endocrine third eye system of consciousness and how to achieve divinity and cosmic consciousness by the balancing of opposites at the apex, indicated by the Golden Pyramid capstone, were duality becomes whole, it becomes one, we have mastered the physical world, with each chakra having first been balanced.

This was so large that its importance could be in no doubt. They wanted to show us how much it meant to them and what value it had been placed upon it, a massive statement in the desert.

And it isn't only Pyramids, many Churches and Cathedrals are also showing the endocrine system when you overlay a figure of the human head over the floor plans of Churches/Cathedrals too. There is such an example at a Cathedral near to my home town called 'Lichfield Cathedral'.

By overlaying the image of the head onto Lichfield it has been found that the eyes looked directly out of the mystical north door (Pineal Gland is known as the 'North Gate').

The centre of the brain the Thalamus is positioned exactly in the centre of the Cathedral. The crown chakra was exactly where the great altar was situated and the throat chakra ran straight up the centre of the Nave (throat chakra deals with communication).

The pineal gland and the pituitary gland were neatly placed under two columns running at 45 degrees to each other. There is truly a greater mystique at play with these sacred buildings.

In Egyptian circles the Halls of Amenti are mentioned, they act as a distortion filter between our physical being and the Soul. It is the realm between the Omega Point and our 3D world. Reincarnation happens from the Halls of Amenti back to the physical body.

The term Omega point stands for the highest level of consciousness.

The Halls of Amenti, the ultimate hall of mirrors, is the realm of the great illusion that is only passable by knowledge and wisdom. After passing the Halls of Amenti merger with the Omega Point follows. The Halls of Amenti are the 'Hidden Mind'!

We have been left in the most grand and significant way the key and path to enlightenment by an advanced race that knew the secrets of body and universe and its connections. Maybe we can follow them into greatness!

"Though I walk through the valley of the shadow of death, I will fear no evil: for thou art with me; thy rod and thy staff they comfort me" – Psalm 23:4

In other words I will face my own inner darkness with the shepherd staff and flailing rod of Osiris; the Egyptian god of the underworld; for my comfort. This was the 'Weighing of the Heart' ceremony and the Judgement of Osiris.

("Thy Rod and Thy Staff", two depictions)

The 'heart' of the soul was handed over to Osiris who placed it on a great golden scale balanced against the white feather of Ma'at, the feather of truth, of harmony, on the other side. If the soul's heart was lighter than the feather then the soul was freely admitted into the bliss of the Field of Reeds. You are as the saying goes 'Light hearted'.

Should the heart prove heavier, however, it was thrown to the floor of the Hall of Truth where it was devoured by the god Amenti. The individual soul then ceased to exist. There was no 'hell' for the ancient Egyptians; their 'fate worse than death' was non-existence.

Consciousness was everything to the hierarchy of Egyptian society and all that they did was working towards the God-state.

10

THE PYRAMID MATRIX –
SUPREME MATHEMATICS...

And the intergalactic Connection

(Numeric References courtesy of Carl Munck). It is not possible sitting in 2017 to say who built the pyramids of not only Egypt but all around planet Earth and even beyond Earth and to the Planet Mars.

It is strange however for a pictorial race who drew and documented everything that they did would not document the building of the Pyramids and Sphinx. Can we therefore say that they did not build them? What is clear when you read this chapter is that there has been an overview, maybe not even from this planet, speaking that universal language of Mathematics. In order to accomplish what you are about to read you have to have a panoramic view of the whole scene and be in a position to coordinate everything with the knowledge of all else involved.

This requires a level of cooperation between cultures and even galactic visitors; a fact denied by any mainstream version of history who tell us that these cultures never met or had any contact between them. This is not at all possible!

The word Mathematics derives from the word Mathema which means to know. When I was at secondary school in the 1980's math's was a boring rendition of algebra and times tables taught by an alcoholic teacher who would go for a drink at lunch time and come back to school and fall asleep in the classroom for the whole lesson, things were different in those days, albeit relatively recent. Suffice to say I didn't learn much by way of numbers. However the make-up of the universe is held within mathematical codes pre-programmed numbers that nature does not deviate from. The Egyptians called this the sound right reason, supreme mathematics and they used mathematical numbers and sequences such as Phi & Fibonacci long before history books tell us they were discovered. The Fibonacci sequence is nature's code from the shell of a snail, to the stabilizing spiral of a flower, to gigantic nebulas; they all adhere to this code. Nature doesn't only relate to Earth's plants, trees and wildlife it extends to the cosmos, the Neteru.

So, it is of no surprise that the Pyramids of Egypt form part of a pyramidal matrix system that connects the great monuments of Earth and even beyond by mathematical coordinates that are quite frankly, mind-blowing.

And most astonishing is that there is a planetary and solar system pyramid matrix system whereby famous monuments refer to each other in their mathematical sizing and locations; by giving the exact locations/coordinates of each other within their diameters. On Earth we have famous monuments put there, or so we believe, by the ancients who knew many secrets to the make-up of the cosmos and they used advanced mathematics to conceal coordinates of other monuments within the numerology of their own monuments and this extends to the planet Mars. Was this a GPS homing system for those from other worldly locations, a guidance system for them to find certain places?

"ALL IS NUMBER" – Pythagorus:

When we look at the make-up of our universe we see that this is correct. From the gas giant spirals of Galaxies to small shells on the beach everything in existence follows a mathematical code to the last number and it doesn't deviate, not even the human foetus as it grows to the 64 Tetrahedron grid in sequences of 8, the Genesis pattern. The physical finite world is governed by finite fractals and the infinite universe is governed by infinite fractals (Duplication).

One of the most remarkable mathematical codes is the Mandelbrot set, a complex series of numbers that will not deviate and can only be replicated by computer, a complex series that is self-replicating according to some predetermined rule. This remarkable sequence also appeared as a crop-circle in the UK in the 1990's.

The Mandelbrot set creates a finite mathematical equation of ZN (The set of complex numbers C for which the iteration $zn+1 = zn2 + C$ produces finite zn for all n when started at $z0 = 0$ – duplicating forever in the none physical world). Some say the abstract concept within the mind of a Pure Mathematician = The Creator! All creation being a flash of instantaneous energy, (thought into physical creation, all programs must have a programmer).

This is known scientifically as the 'One Time Beginning' to the general population as the 'Big Bang Theory' proven by the COBE Experiment (Cosmic Background Explorer, a satellite sent to the extremities of space between 1989-1993)

The universe as are ourselves are number sequences and everything in the existence of all things relate to a number in some capacity.

So let's analyse the mathematics between monuments and societies that we are taught were primitive. We use Greenwich in London as our time meridian, this is incorrect, the real Meridian is the Great Pyramid in Giza, the exact center of all landmass of Earth. These monuments are all connected by Grid-Vectors from Mexico and Peru, to England and Egypt and beyond that too. Imagine a time where there is no sound, no light and nothingness rules the universe.

All that exists is an abstract concept of pure mathematics, encoded number sequences, finite and infinite fractals that will later form shapes and instructions to give us the building blocks of life. Then all at once a 'One Time Beginning' a Eureka moment, a flash of energy and light, the Big bang and then the universe houses life as we know it. Massless particles, light, slow down as they travel through Higgs Field and turn into mass, causing condensed light to form physicality. Sub-atomic particles travel back and forwards in time, the duration of existence that will become pinnacle in our third dimensional reality. We are made of the same sub-atomic particles and can therefore also time travel and this gives rise to the going back to our past and forwards into our future, a quantum tunnelling effect.

We are in effectively in many places at the same time living out multi-dimensionality contributing to the every possibility mix, all different actions of the same event but as a parallel, resulting in a different conclusion.

Dimensions, the minimum amount of coordinates required to specify a point within; provide rooms within the dodecahedron system and wavelengths separate life forms behind a small veil of frequency spectra so that they remain unseen but for a brief glimpse as they tune in to one another.

The Russian doll of micro macro trickles down to you and I as I sit here writing and you sit there reading, but nevertheless we are an intricate part of the whole experiencing every possibility until all returns to the whole once again, perfection knows little without hands-on experience. We skip from one block of third dimensional time to another which in order to continue to function as dimensionality must have a definitive separation which is our life and death cycle, the transition from linear to lateral time, a change of viewpoint as the movie slides that are our life flicker from one scene to the next.
As humans in modern society we tend to journey through life blinkered, told by our media and our religions that this is it, we have one life and then we become senseless and non-existent for eternity.

NOW TIME FOR THE ASTONISHING MATHS:

Stonehenge in Wiltshire, UK, is a 360 degree circle that has 60 outer stones and 15 center blocks. When we use the mathematical formula 360 x 60 it equals 21,600 which is a multiple of 51 degrees divided by 10 divided by 42.35 (51 degrees + 10 minutes + 42,35 seconds) this is the exact location of Stonehenge. 2160 is also in years the age of the zodiac sign transition, each sign rules for that period of time.

Stonehenge is 288 feet across which when multiplied by PI and multiplied by 15 (center block number) divided by the square root 15 we get 52,562 which is the exact grid longitude of Stonehenge. 52,562 divided by 360 PI = a square root of 2160. Square root 2160 divided by 2 PI = the grid reference of the 3 smaller Pyramids in Egypt (adjacent to the Great Pyramid et al) which equals the square root 2.71 which is the megalithic yard (2.72 also known as Euler's Number).

360 divided by the Megalithic yard squared = the radius of the Great Pyramid itself.

When we use the 3 dimensional formation of the Great Pyramid using double PI we get 9929.184896 which is the encoded grid latitude of the Pyramid of Cydonian City on Planet Mars. And in addition to this the famous face on

Mars has a grid latitude of 4523.893421 which when divided by the square root 2160 equals 97.3386882 which is the diameter of Stonehenge (The Moon has a diameter of 2159 miles, extremely close to this number).

The Cydonian city on Mars is also an exact map overlay of Avebury in Wiltshire, UK. You have to ask how this is possible.

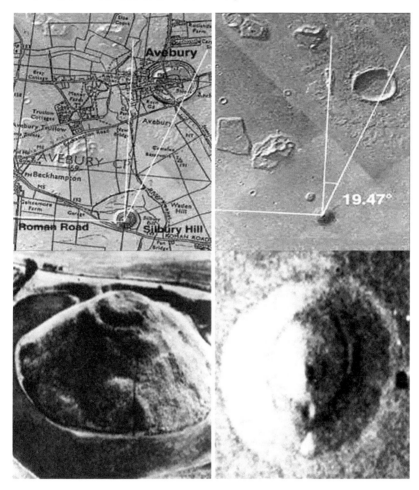

(Avebury & Cydonia on Mars)

This correlation between encoded mathematical coordinates also extends to other Pyramids too such as in Mexico and elsewhere as well as other monuments/sacred locations around the globe. We have a complex yet beautiful system of coded mathematics of the advanced level that we arrogantly believe is patented by modern science; we are very much wrong.

All Within All - NUMBER 9

And here are a few more examples of the universal relevance of the number 9 in addition to what I have also previously mentioned. 9ether forces of creation = The one time beginning, the number 9... The foetus spends 9 months in the womb and atoms are 99.9% empty space, 9 to the 9th power of 9, it is a significant number. 9 is the last single number and also the last double number and triple number. The number 9 is the all-encompassing circle of creation itself.

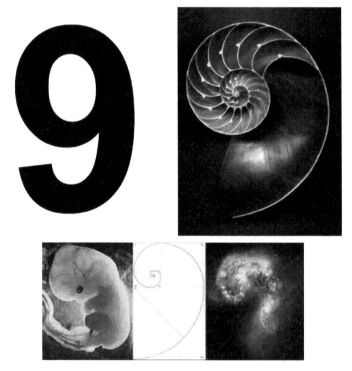

(Number 9; the all-encompassing circle of creation itself present within the foetus, the Fibonacci sequence, the universe and the Nautilus Shell...)

It's time to put down our school text books and learn the truth. Sound Right Reason, the Supreme Mathematics that Pythagoras stated we must know In order to connect to God, GOD meaning the 'Geometry Of Divinity' or sacred Geometry, Earth Measure! On that basis God and his Angels soon becomes God and his Angles...

11

CONCLUSION:
The Battle For Eden (The Human Body)

Now that you are at the end of the book and you have been shown some real revelations that have been hidden from you regarding yourself and your own greatness and the rest of humanity throughout our time here on Earth; is it any wonder that the powers that be, the same powers that have retained this information for themselves, try at all costs to keep you ignorant and deny you salvation? What the establishment does effectively is to place information of truth in so many different places under different guises, a schism effect, that most people cannot or will never find it, it has been cleverly concealed for that reason.

(The apple and the Garden of Eden; Eden being the Human body)

What I have done with this book and others is to reverse that trend, defragging in computer terms, bringing everything back to a central place accessible to everyone who wants to find it and providing one central place in which it can be easily found. Our two dualistic aspects must come back to the same place for us to move forwards as beings, information known by the ancient and advanced Egyptians. The Egyptians knew that the thing that brings duality into balance is a third party which then creates the trinity.

The very same aristocracy and our shadow people behind the establishment, who do this, as a result of this esoteric knowledge, know the workings of the human body and how it connects to a higher place. They know that we are vibratory beings, that we are a smaller universe as are atoms within us, that we are solar systems and universes for, all within all. They know that if they can keep us in one aspect of ourselves we can never reach enlightenment and that is their very intent. They are holding back the development of humanity and they need to go.

They know that as humans we need certain life essential things such as water and food and oxygen in the air to breath and this is of course their way into our sacred Garden, 'The Garden of Eden' and they intend to stunt any growth within that garden, the establishment are our weed-killer so to speak.

It takes just a little research and a little time to figure out how they are doing it and how they are attacking our bodies in order to keep us in a low and harmful vibrational state. GMO's in food that genetically modify our DNA, the likes of fluoride and other additives in water that destroy our pineal glands by calcification and Geoengineering (Chemtrails) in our atmosphere that contain harmful metals that eventually land on our crops that end up on our dinner plates that we hastily eat in our fast paced lives. These air-borne tactics also flood the air with clusters of Positive Ions, which despite their name are not positive; they do in fact cause lethargy and sickness when clustered in great numbers. Chemtrails (bio-engineering) also contain Aluminum which blocks a pyramids energy field this is relevant to our own pyramid which was highlighted in the Egyptian chapter. And subsequently our strive for greater consciousness.

We have a system that creates stress and division with our monetary debt based control and we are always at odds because we believe that it is right to kill to prove that our God is the most peaceful.

We have a global and contrived system of control namely religion that treats women as a lesser being, making them cover their heads with the likes of the Hijab which means to partition, to divide. They are symbolically cutting off their crown chakra from the cosmic consciousness. We are told by our religions that we can only get to God through them; this is of course a fake canopy of fraud perpetrated on the masses.

Your religions should instead be teaching you that there is a deepness beyond the comprehension of most people, from the unconscious followers of religion to the general masses.

There has been many ancient civilizations who somehow knew these magnificent secrets and held universal knowledge, such as the ancient Egyptians, who told us esoterically through their Gods, far greater than anything known today by the masses and even religious Guru's. Hell, that word used to threaten us into compliance is 'Life On Earth'.

A psycho-physical (Body & Mind = Testament) spark of universal consciousness channelled through the Sun (Jesus/heavenly being) which then enters into the unconscious physical material flesh to self-experience, the burial of the soul, or as the Egyptians called it, Mummification, the sleep-state, the Karast (Krst = Christ/Burial), a universal principle implanted into unconscious matter (Matter = Material/physicality = condensed light as it goes through Higgs Field and vibrationally slows down) Jesus into a physical existence!

In the alphabet the Christ is hidden with the letters QRSTU. The first letter 'A', means Aleph (meaning the father), which is Jesus and God.

So Jesus did the will of God = The Wheel of Gad (Zodiac, 12 signs = 12 disciples of Jesus/Sun) and the Lord's Prayer tells us that 'Thy Will shall be done on Earth as it is in Heaven', which is the harmonisation and synchronisation between conscious thought and the subconscious mind; mind and matter.

The teachings we are bound by are superficial that do tell us the true origins of ourselves, if we dig deep enough, but are hidden by cleverly written stories that throw us completely off the scent, just as intended. This is what your priests and religions should really be teaching you. Religion keeps you from knowing your own divinity and mind by the promise of reward or the fear of punishment.

We have a political system of illusion.

Nazareth, that Biblical place which means Priest-Kings, has certain relevance even today. There has always been a Religious connection to Kings, politics and power; all go hand in hand both historically and in the modern day which is no different.

Many American citizens do not know that in 1871 their constitution was superseded by Lex Fori (Law of the Forum) which is Roman Vatican Law, and the Potus (President, which also means Celebrant of Eucharist/Holy Communion) is Vassal King, holder of land answerable to the British Monarchy who in turn are answerable to the Vatican.

Rome has a senate in Capitoline Hill and America has a senate in Capitol Hill! Both have the Eagle as their symbol, the word America also means 'Rule of the eternal Eagle, or the eternal Eagle's rule'. America is a corporation and the US President is CEO of that corporation. "Presidents are selected, not elected" – Roosevelt.

The world is much, much different to what we are told, the power strings are controlled by and attached to the hands of those we don't ever see.

Elections are not an act of fairness or democracy; they are an illusion, created to give the impression of a democracy. Don't be fooled, your liberty depends upon it. And for those currently rioting over the loss of this electoral illusion, you are one of the reasons that humanity is in the mess it currently is!

We live in a world of fake reality.

Since the dawn of our history knowledge and wisdom has been seen as a gift and not a right and as such only the privileged few have been entitled to it, likened to a seed beneath the ground concealed as it grows sprouting in only the minds of the few. The masses on the other hand deliberately kept in the dark so that this seed of knowledge could never grow in their particular garden, starved of the 'Light' another phrase meaning knowledge.

Imagine an invisible prison, a prison that has no walls and no gates and yet no one try's to escape for the simple reason they don't know that they live in a prison. Imagine a race of beings so great they are the universe incarnate with all its infinite energy and atomic particles and genetic makeup and yet they have not one clue of their greatness because it has been hidden from their consciousness for generation after generation.

Then come to the realisation that I am referring to planet Earth and the human race, yes ourselves and our home, but how?

A system put in place so genius and interwoven into the fabric of our reality that those, the minority who see it, are seen by the rest of society as lacking certain minerals when it comes to sanity, the laughing stock to be singled out and mocked and ridiculed and in our recent past even executed as heretics.
We are faced with a hidden language that is encoded all around us that we never decipher, hidden in corporate logos and brand names and alike and by public mudras that only the initiates can understand.

Then we are faced with the most genius creation to date, Religion, and its divide and conquer triumphs over humanity as a race of beings even taking us beyond the point of genocide and war in the name of a so called loving God! Somehow bypassing our ability to think and consider just what it is we're doing to each other, flicking off the switch of basic humanity and mental rationale, such is its allowed power over us.

Keeping in line with self-aggrandisement the masses have been given false messiahs and idols of worship, a physical storyline to dictate their lives instead of taking ownership and taking appropriate moral actions, choosing to pass the responsibility to another deity to cure all sin and ills which has played right into the hands of the deceivers. It has taken us outside ourselves instead of within which is where our greatness resides, our own Temple (House of God) and Golgotha, the place of skulls where we find the human Brain, the Ark of the Covenant, our cosmic connection.

It is important for a regime intent on the global control of people and resources achieved by ignorance to keep certain information relating to our own greatness away from us for obvious reasons, namely if we all knew how brilliant we really were they would no longer hold claim on us and our lives. If we took control of ourselves and didn't need a deity in the sky to rescue us they would have no carrot of reward and no stick of punishment to persuade us to follow them.

Religion is the basis of that control and it is powerful. People are sold physical people and stories when in fact at a much deeper level of understanding the Bible and alike are really taking about astronomy and human genetics and how they act in synergy under 'Medical Astronomy', it is an ascension book, a secret knowledge withheld from us all.

The world is not how we have been brought up to believe, the things we celebrate, the things we do, the things we have for so long believed in are merely a cloud, a distraction, a deceitful lie imposed upon us all for many millenniums by the masters of fabrication.

Our entertainment (enter and contain the mind) industries such as advertisements which actually means to Entice Adversity into our mind, and our music which had its Hertz changed to a deliberate inharmonious frequency to harm us (Hertz = amount of oscillations per second- Music = Mu, negative and sic, a consequence = a negative consequence) all add to keeping us down and docile; a million and one distractions to stop us from ever thinking. Minds rented out to phones and irrelevant things so that we never have time to think about the bigger picture, of which we are all a frame.

We are beings of amazing potential. We are universal power ready to be awoken. We are all part of the all-encompassing one time beginning having an experience here at this time. Our true essence is riding within the empty spaces of the atom of our slow vibrating body like a letter takes a ride in its envelope; pre- destined and pre –addressed by its sender.

Don't be a carpet for anyone or any system that wants to keep you at ground level, reach for your rightful place, the stars, armed with your rightful inheritance, knowledge!

As I've previously stated that during the writing of this book strange things have happened to me. I have seen cobalt blue scarab beetles morphing in my house and I have seen serpent shaped pure light slithering away from my left foot at speed until it disappeared seconds later and I have had headache pain in the region of my third eye. When we delve into Egypt and the Egyptian principles of enlightenment we get opened up just as they did all those millenniums ago. Enlightenment will become manifest with the re-emergence of Egyptian knowledge.

Much of the information in this book has come from places beyond our dimension, it is very much multidimensional as were the Egyptians themselves. The Mayans told us about our self with their pyramids of 9 steps which represented the 9 stages of consciousness, the Greeks with their Gods of Olympus, symbolic of our God self that needs acknowledgement in order to become the furness of fire it has the potential to be. And of course the Egyptians told us these things by means of what you have already read in this book, our hidden internal fire, the God energy. They are all in their own way telling us one thing, that being, about our own God-State!

And with regards to the Riddle of the Sphinx at the beginning of the book, well the answer was... *'Man'!*, which has been the theme throughout this book. What walks on four legs in the morning *(child/baby crawling on all fours)* On Two legs in the afternoon *(Man upright on two legs)* Three legs in the evening *(old man with a stick)* and no legs at night *(a dead man unable to walk)*... MAN!

Best wishes until we all meet again as one power. If you have any questions then I can be contacted via the contact form on my website.

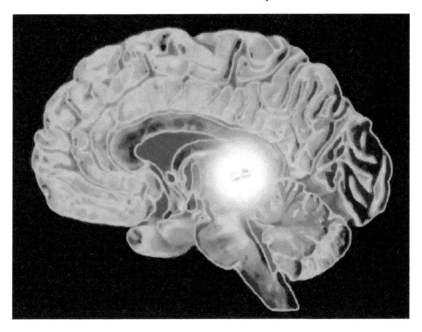

"The pen is mightier than the sword", pen in etymology (which is the history of words), means 'head'. Therefore the mind is more powerful than any weapon.

Best regards and best of luck!

Michael Feeley
www.michael-feeley.com

OTHER TITLES BY MICHAEL FEELEY

PAPERBACKS

Walk Into The Light – The Journey Of A Lightworker Duo
ISBN; 978-0-9566103-0-0
Beyond The Illusion – A Time Of Awakening
ISBN; 978-0-9566103-1-7
Earth Is An Experiment, Duality Is A Game... And Love Is The Answer
ISBN; 978-0-9566103-2-4
The Secret of Christ
ISBN; 978-0-9954554-5-0

EBOOKS

7 Things The Police Don't Want You To Know
ISBN; 978-0-9954554-6-7
Police Encounters of the Third Kind
ISBN; 978-0-9954554-7-4
When Murder Travels Through Time
ISBN; 978-0-9954554-8-1
Stonehenge - The Secret Of The Monoliths
ISBN; 978-1-912400-02-7

Available to purchase from
www.michael-feeley.com

Michael Presents His Talk, 'The Ancient Code'

If you would like Michael to speak at your venue please get in touch via his website: www.michael-feeley.com

Self-Publishing Your Book Made Easy!

Michael's Publisher Sazmick Books, offer self-publishing, editing and marketing services to authors of most genres. We help to fulfill your ambition of getting your work from typed or written manuscript, into a printed book or E-book with customisable add-ons.

Simple packages, Stunning books.

Chat with us and get your book on the road today!

www.sazmickbooks.com

For All Your Self-Publishing Needs

BV - #0099 - 291221 - C8 - 210/148/10 - PB - 9780995455443 - Gloss Lamination